Lord Carlingford's Journal

Chichester Fortescue, Lord Carlingford (About 1886)

Lord Carlingford's Journal

Reflections of a Cabinet Minister
1885

EDITED BY

A. B. COOKE
RESEARCH FELLOW, THE QUEEN'S UNIVERSITY OF BELFAST

and

J. R. VINCENT
PROFESSOR OF MODERN HISTORY, THE UNIVERSITY OF BRISTOL

CLARENDON PRESS · OXFORD

1971

Oxford University Press, Ely House, London W. 1

GLASGOW NEW YORK TORONTO MELBOURNE WELLINGTON
CAPE TOWN SALISBURY IBADAN NAIROBI DAR ES SALAAM LUSAKA ADDIS ABABA
BOMBAY CALCUTTA MADRAS KARACHI LAHORE DACCA
KUALA LUMPUR SINGAPORE HONG KONG TOKYO

PRINTED IN GREAT BRITAIN
BY THE ABERDEEN UNIVERSITY PRESS

ACKNOWLEDGEMENTS

WE are indebted to Her Majesty the Queen for her gracious permission to consult the Royal Archives, and for allowing certain passages to be cited.

We wish to express our deep gratitude to Lord Strachie, the owner of the MSS. on which this edition is based, for placing the papers of Lord Carlingford at the disposal of scholars, and for giving his approval to the idea of publishing an edition of the journal. We hope that this edition is worthy of his generosity.

The papers of Lord Carlingford are now in the care of Somerset County Record Office, Taunton. We would like to thank Mr. Collis, the County Archivist, and his staff, for their kind co-operation.

We are glad to acknowledge the generous advice given by Mr. C. H. D. Howard of Queen Mary College, London, and also the encouragement we have received from Mr. John Brooke, of the Historical Manuscripts Commission, and Professor M. R. D. Foot, of the University of Manchester.

Finally, our thanks are due to the Delegates of the Oxford University Press, not only for being ready to publish material of rather unusual character, but for the freedom they have allowed us in choosing how to present that material.

CONTENTS

INTRODUCTION

THE Cabinet is the least understood institution in British politics. Since Victorian Cabinets kept no formal records, the diaries of the period which record Cabinet proceedings have a unique value for the study of British central government. Such informal records as were kept (e.g. Gladstone's personal notes and his letters to the Queen) cannot rival the work of the diarists, for they neither constitute an adequate administrative record of decisions reached, nor do they give enlightenment as to the internal political situation in the Cabinet.

However, of the diaries and letters already printed, none gives a continuous view of what went on in Cabinet meetings. The edition of Kimberley's journal for 1868–74,[1] the correspondence of Gladstone and Granville,[2] the *Letters of Queen Victoria,* the correspondence between the Queen and Gladstone,[3] between the Queen and Palmerston,[4] and that between Palmerston and Gladstone,[5] all throw a great deal of light on the attendant circumstances of Cabinet government, but do not lift the veil from the meetings themselves. Lord Carlingford's journal[6] in this respect stands in a class by itself so far as published material is concerned. One can go further, and claim that it compares favourably with the unpublished political diaries of the period as well.

Carlingford was well suited for the role of diarist. He had little

---

[1] Kimberley, John, 1st Earl of, *A journal of events during the Gladstone ministry, 1868–74,* ed. E. Drus, Camden Miscellany, vol. 21, part ii (London, 1958).

[2] *The Political Correspondence of Mr Gladstone and Lord Granville 1868–1876,* 2 vols. (Oxford, 1952), and *The Political Correspondence of Mr Gladstone and Lord Granville 1876–1886,* 2 vols. (Oxford, 1962), both ed. Agatha Ramm.

[3] *The Queen and Mr Gladstone. A selection from their correspondence,* ed. P. Guedalla (London, 1933).

[4] Brian Connell, *Regina v. Palmerston. The Correspondence between Queen Victoria and Her Foreign and Prime Minister 1837–1865* (London, 1962).

[5] *Gladstone and Palmerston. The Correspondence of Lord Palmerston with Mr Gladstone, 1851–1865,* ed. P. Guedalla (London, 1928).

[6] The original journal is in the Strachie MSS., Strachie: Carlingford, H. 360, in Somerset County Record Office, Taunton.

to do in the way of departmental work or speaking in the House of Lords, so that Cabinet meetings were virtually the sole events of his week. He was exceptionally detached from the cabals within the Cabinet, and had a fine literary intellect and a good eye for motive and character.

There were other diarists at this time dealing up to a point with Cabinet matters, but Carlingford has a fair claim to pride of place. Disregarding the diaries by Edward Hamilton and by Harcourt's son as being based on secondhand information,[1] one is left with Kimberley, Rosebery, and Northbrook. These three Liberal ministers certainly kept diaries: but (as with Gladstone's diaries, now being edited), there is little reason to suppose that any of them will provide an intelligible interpretative account of cabinet proceedings when they become fully available to scholars. One is left with Dilke's unpublished memoirs,[2] written in 1891 on the basis of contemporary diaries and letters. Thus, though these memoirs are largely in diary form, and tend to give a fuller record of minor business taken in Cabinet than Carlingford does, they are not a contemporary record, and they suffer from the same pitfalls as the rest of the Dilke papers as regards subsequent excisions by more than one hand. Further, Dilke's reports of Cabinets reflect his partisan interests and his official concern to establish an exact record of minor foreign policy decisions taken, at the expense of reflection on the political situation inside the Cabinet.

On the Conservative side, the only Cabinet minister who kept a regular journal at this time was Lord Cranbrook: but he found little occasion to describe what went on in the Cabinet, and preferred to write about the weather.

[1] Hamilton's diaries are in the British Museum: at the time of writing an edition of the section dealing with 1880–5 was being prepared for publication. A carefully edited version of Lewis Harcourt's diary, prepared for his father's biographer A. G. Gardiner, is at Stanton Harcourt in Oxfordshire. The original diary appears to be missing.

[2] For the memoirs, see B.M. Add. MSS. 43930–41. They nominally cover 1843–1910, but seven of the volumes relate to the 1880s. For Dilke's diaries, see B.M. Add. MSS. 43924–8. Substantial sections of both memoirs and diaries have been published, somewhat inaccurately, in Gwynn and Tuckwell's biography of Dilke.

Carlingford's journal probably does not bring to light any very startling isolated discovery. It indicates how and why the Liberal ministry of 1880–5 was precarious before, and apart from, the problem of Home Rule, and throws much light on non-Irish factors which contributed to the split of 1886. The journal also establishes how much ministers wished to be defeated in May–June 1885, and the importance of coercion in Ireland as an issue which could break a government. Above all, it provides plentiful examples of political conversation and of the calculations which lay behind actions in Cabinet. It contains incidentally a certain amount of constitutional information about the way business was done in Cabinet.[1]

Carlingford's journal therefore provides one of the best pictures we have of how government by discussion actually works, how discussion develops into policy: and, by coincidence, it does so for an exceptionally important year in English party history.

Chichester Fortescue, Lord Carlingford (1823–98), was an Irish protestant landlord whose life came to centre in his political activities at Westminster and in the care of his estates in England. His claims to fame are three: he sat in two of Gladstone's Cabinets (1868–74, 1880–5), he played a leading part in the passage of the two great Irish Land Acts of 1870 and 1881, and he was the husband of the leading hostess of the Liberal Party, Frances, Dowager Countess Waldegrave, whom he married in 1863. He cannot be called a successful politician by the standards of the assertive professionalism that prevailed in his party. He did nothing badly, he did several things very well: but, unforgivably, he somehow did not seem to matter. In 1885 he was possibly the least important member of the Cabinet. His diaries matter because they were those of a born diarist, not because of what he was as a politician.

[1] As the editors are at present working on a detailed political history of the years 1885–6, which will contain a full discussion of the points arising from the journal, only a brief summary of main trends at this time is given below (see pp. 30–3 below).

Chichester Samuel Fortescue (known as Parkinson-Fortescue[1] from 1861) was born into the lower reaches of the Irish ascendancy on 18 January 1823 at his family home in co. Louth. He was therefore in 1885 older than any other member of the Cabinet except Gladstone, Granville, and Selborne. His mother was the daughter of a Cork barrister: his father, though a lieutenant-colonel and M.P. for Hillsborough in the last Irish Parliament, was plainly of small means, belonging to a cadet branch of an ancient titled family. Prospects for Chichester Fortescue and his elder brother Thomas were therefore limited till the death of a distant relative in 1833, when the senior branch of the family became extinct. The old family title of Viscount Clermont had disappeared, but substantial estates passed to Thomas Fortescue, thus opening the doors of territorial politics to the two brothers.

The inheritance transformed their position. The Fortescue estates were estimated in 1883 to comprise 23,265 acres of Irish land yielding £18,086 a year, most of the land being in co. Louth. How the 1883 figures related to the position in the 1840s is not known, but as regards territorial standing there cannot have been much difference. On this foundation both brothers set out to weave their dreams, Thomas setting his sights on the restoration of the family title, Chichester on social and political distinction.

Chichester however first achieved success in a quite different walk of life. Though he did not attend public school, his Oxford career brought him an aura of distinction. He made lifelong friends. He also gained a first in *lit. hum.*, the Chancellor's English essay prize,[2] a studentship of Christ Church (1843–56) which was renewed as an honorary studentship in 1867, and a sympathy for literature and speculation ranging far beyond the old classical curriculum. His range of reading was quite remarkable. His

[1] See Irish Genealogical Office MS. 152, pp. 352–5, for copy of royal licence to take the name of Parkinson in addition to and before the name Fortescue, 29 Oct. 1861.

[2] *Effects of the Conquest of England by the Normans. An Essay read in the Theatre, Oxford, June 24, 1846.*

recorded reading during 1885, a year when he could hardly have been further from feeling intellectually energetic, was as follows: Maine's *Early Law*, Renan's *Prêtre de Némi*, Dean Church's *Bacon*, Huxley's *Hume*, the medieval *Ancren Riwle*, Aelfric, Mill's *Essays on Religion*, Rossetti's verse, Morley's *Voltaire*, Green's *Prolegomena*, Arnold's *Literature and Dogma*, Herbert Spencer's *Principles*, Lessing's plays, Tylor on anthropology, Farrer's *Fair Trade*, Renan's *Souvenirs*, Sweet's *Early English Primer*, Renan's *Marc Aurèle*, *Romola*, Mill's *Logic*, Mill on Hamilton, Lessing's essay *Leibniz von dem Ewigen Strafen*, Blunt's *Dictionary of Sects*, Cross's *Life of George Eliot*, Feuerbach's *Essence of Christianity*, novels by George Sand, Ouida, and Balzac, memoirs by Croker, Greville and Sir H. Taylor, Trollope's *Autobiography* (when ill in bed), the periodical *Deutsche Rundschau*[1] on Darwinism, Martineau on ethics, 'a Latin grammar and a German reading book', and various publications of the Historical Manuscripts Commission, on which he served. Also in 1885 he talked to his official subordinates, T. H. Huxley and Matthew Arnold, with interest, sympathy, and pleasure. There was no doubt about his fitness for academic pursuits or his ability to meditate. So far as he had a central intellectual interest, it was in discussions of religion as observed from the outside.

Oxford not only sharpened him into a natural intellectual, it initiated him into the Whig view of the world. He lost the old beliefs of childhood, such as an evangelical home provided, and did not acquire any new commitments. From his college days he he took the line that traditional Whig views of Church and State would be found to mix well with the most advanced speculations of the day. The intellectual tragedy of his life was that Whig politicians had no more taste for civilized and bookish speculation than did any other men of their trade. Indeed, they might well by deep conviction have grounds for dismissing such attainments. Northbrook, who was probably Carlingford's closest friend in the political world, was the humble author of *The Teaching of Jesus Christ in His Own Words*, a text for distribution

---

[1] Fortescue spent four months in Dresden in 1846 learning German.

to the natives of India in their own languages: whereas Carlingford's maiden speech was against Jewish disabilities, and his
first pamphlet[1] argued the same theme of the secular nature of
the State.

It was either at or through Christ Church that he made his own
main male friendships. These, three in number, stood the test of
years remarkably well. There was Alfred Seymour, the un-
ambitious Somerset country gentleman: Henry Grenfell, banker,
gossip, and man of the world, with whom Carlingford shared
rooms in St. James's Place in 1853–63: and Lord Northbrook,
solemn, thoughtful, and pious, and not obviously a fellow spirit
for this circle of Christ Church contemporaries. But the small circle
lasted: when Northbrook went off to be viceroy of India, it was
Carlingford, Grenfell, and two other college friends with whom
he breakfasted prior to departure. 'There is a deep melancholy in
him, but a strong sense of duty and a sincere feeling for his friends'
Carlingford then wrote of Northbrook, who was more than ever
a man of sorrows following the death of his wife in 1867 and the
drowning of his son in the *Captain* in 1870. In intellectual matters
Carlingford and Northbrook were incompatible: in politics there
was a remarkable identity of view, and their view of themselves
as committed widowers strengthened their disposition to seek
each other's company, though they were a little at a loss when
actually together.

A fifth figure fairly soon became a member of the group, none
other than the famous illustrator and humorist, Edward Lear
(1812–88) who met Fortescue ('40-skew' to Lear) in Italy in 1845.
Initially captivated by Fortescue's brilliance, Lear became an
accepted figure in his circle. In 1848, for instance, he met Northbrook—a 'luminous and amiable brick' said Lear—who, when
viceroy of India, employed Lear as his artist in residence. Similarly,
not only Fortescue, but also Lady Waldegrave, treated Lear as a
political confidant to a quite surprising degree. Carlingford and
Lear kept up a steady correspondence over a generation, which,

---

[1] *Christian Profession not the Test of Citizenship. An Essay for the Day* (London, 1849).

even if only of mild interest, still shows a capacity for easy friendship on both sides,[1] lasting till Lear's death.

By 1885 Carlingford was seeing much more of his college friends of the 1840s, than of his Whig political friends, and much more of both than of Whig 'society'. The only politician to whom he offered hospitality in 1885 was Mundella, whose manner he found irritating and who certainly was no Whig: nor did Carlingford, throughout the year, attend a single country house party dedicated to political confabulation. He spent as many nights as possible in Somerset, even if it meant commuting to London for Cabinets: and when he was resident in London, it was frequently to see his relatives, rather than to be in the political world.

In general, Whigs had no particular liking for other Whigs, especially at ministerial level. They knew each other too well to like or respect each other. Carlingford, after 1879, was perhaps only exceptional in that his opportunities of making contact with other politicians through his job were unusually small. But it is quite clear that there was no Whig world for him to be a member of: just a world of Whig administrators with their heads in their files.

Carlingford's scanty correspondence with Granville, the party leader most favourably inclined to him in 1881-5, confirms what one might expect: that from time to time Carlingford could count on being listened to, as an intermediary who could smooth things over with the Queen; as the possessor of an uncertain amount of expertise on Irish questions; as a critical intelligence naturally at home in analysing, without affecting, issues of imperial statesmanship. What is not revealed, and almost certainly did not exist, was a common partisanship for Whiggery, the *esprit de corps* of sect, class, or party which in the public mind bound these men together.

In almost every case the papers left by members of the 1880-5

[1] Lady Strachey, ed., *Letters of Edward Lear, Author of 'The Book of Nonsense', to Chichester Fortescue, Lord Carlingford, and Frances Countess Waldegrave* (2 vols., London, 1907). Enquiries failed to locate any relevant papers left by Seymour or Grenfell. Northbrook's papers only came to light, in unsorted form, while this book was at the printers, and it is still too early to say whether Northbrook's political papers for 1885 have survived, although first indications are unpromising.

Cabinet contain no correspondence with Carlingford during the last year or so of the ministry. In any particular collection this might imply selective destruction: over a wide range of archives, it implies that Carlingford was, as he said, a very isolated figure by 1885. The Devonshire MSS. show that Carlingford neither looked to nor won support or intimacy from Hartington, even in 1885–6 when they were bound by obvious ties, as 'Palmerstonians' in international and imperial policy, and Unionists in Irish policy.

It is particularly the absence of any regular correspondence from those like Granville and Hartington, people sympathetic to him on issues of current politics, that establishes his isolation. His opinion was not canvassed, even to pick up an odd vote in Cabinet. Spencer, with whom he worked closely in 1868–70, only received an occasional letter from Carlingford, whose own archives contain nothing from Spencer after 1883. In the whole of 1885, Carlingford appears to have written not more than perhaps a dozen letters to all his cabinet colleagues put together. The common verdict was put by Harcourt after he had had Carlingford down for the weekend:

He does not really recover at all as his life had been so absorbed in Lady W. that he has left himself no reserve of attachments.[1]

In 1885 Carlingford lived in three worlds: the lost world of Lady Waldegrave, the still satisfying world of informal friendships and absorbing intellectual interests kept alive from his time at Oxford, and, perhaps least real of the the three to him, the world of Cabinet politics, which had so failed to bring him any close attachments. It was this failure which hurt him most about politics, not the fact of the inevitable delays and disappointments of his career, which in its way had been satisfying and productive enough.

In 1847 he was returned at the general election for his native county of Louth. He held the seat without interruption till 1874—no mean feat in itself. To have sat in the House of Commons at

[1] Harcourt to Rosebery, 22 Aug. 1882; Rosebery MSS., box 26.

all distinguished him sharply enough from those who had always been peers pure and simple like Spencer and Rosebery: to have held an Irish popular constituency for a generation indicated an ability to survive in an Irish context which no other Victorian Cabinet minister could rival. The fact that he successfully opposed the Irish movement of the 1850s may have influenced his view of the Irish party of the 1880s.

His main object while an Irish member was not, however, to build up a power base in Ireland, nor in any sense to act as the local head of the Liberal Party, but to climb the rungs of a metropolitan career. That he was pained by the problems of Ireland, in a most generous way, is as clear as that he saw them essentially from London and from the point of view of a political career with which he expected and hoped Ireland would have nothing to do. Little material remains as to the extent of his political associations in Ireland outside the limits of his constituency and of the Castle administration. But only briefly, and then only by accidents of the political breeze, did he figure as a politician especially involved in Irish affairs.

Entering Parliament in the same year as he took his M.A., Fortescue had obviously to mark time before promotion offered itself. Either his own services, or his brother's donations to party funds, sufficed to secure an Irish peerage for his brother in 1852, but his own turn did not come till 1854, when he became a junior whip under Aberdeen.[1] Under the succeeding Palmerston ministry, he was temporarily out of office, but returned in 1857-8 as Under-Secretary at the Colonial Office, a place which he again occupied in 1859-65. In 1857-8 and 1859-64 his superior was the Duke of Newcastle, so that Fortescue bore the brunt in the lower house, and therefore had all the more to resent when, on Newcastle's death, he was in effect relegated by the appointment of a commoner, Cardwell, as Colonial Secretary. Another point to recall

---

[1] For the early phase of his career, see '. . . *and Mr Fortescue': A Selection from the Diaries from 1851 to 1862 of Chichester Fortescue, Lord Carlingford*, ed. O. Wyndham Hewett (London, 1958). There is no evidence that any further journals kept by Carlingford in later life have survived, though Carlingford in 1885 refers to one such volume covering the year 1884.

is that Newcastle was, by the standards of the day and in an old sense of the word, quite a convinced 'imperialist', so that when Carlingford in his journal shows consistent signs of 'thinking imperially' in 1885, it may be more correct to interpret this in terms of his experience in the 1860s, than to refer it to the *Zeitgeist* of the 1880s.

Under Palmerston, Fortescue was at most very slowly achieving seniority, and building up a claim, at least in his own mind, to the reversion to the Colonial Office.[1] The family collection of consolatory and nominal awards increased, Fortescue getting a P.C. when passed over in 1864, and an Irish P.C. in 1866, while his brother, Lord Clermont, was promoted to a U.K. peerage, also in 1866, in addition to the Irish title he had been given in 1852. His performance in Parliament was neither impressive nor unimpressive. His problem lay elsewhere, in his representing no dominant body of sentiment.

Palmerston's death changed all this. Fortescue was on one level a Russell man: on another level, he exactly fitted the needs of a Liberal party which was changing from a 'Protestant' to a 'Catholic' alignment in Ireland. That change required the dismissal of Sir R. Peel, Palmerston's brusque Irish Secretary, and his replacement with a more attractive figure.[2]

Fortescue's first term as Chief Secretary for Ireland (Nov. 1865–June 1866) offered him little scope, particularly as the Lord-Lieutenant, Wodehouse, was in the Cabinet, and Fortescue was not—an exclusion he treated as a great grievance in letters to Russell and Wodehouse. Yet, although executive action against the Fenians dominated Irish affairs, he managed to introduce a land bill, designed to allow tenants compensation for improvements.

---

[1] For Fortescue's thinking about promotion, see his remark in 1861, when he came very near to getting the Irish office. 'I told the Duke [of Newcastle] how I disliked the Irish office and had always wished to keep out of it... He said I might naturally look and was "fully entitled" to be head of the Colonial Office one of these days.' (Hewett, '. . . *and Mr Fortescue*', p. 182).

[2] In 1886 the situation was reversed. Sir R. Peel was then the only Tory to vote for the Home Rule Bill, doing so at great personal sacrifice: while Carlingford was one of few unequivocal and disinterested opponents in the Liberal ranks. At the 1886 general election, Peel unsuccessfully contested a Scottish seat as a home ruler.

The defeat of the 1866 Reform Bill and the fall of the Liberal government caused the measure to be dropped. His solitary glory at this time was that his good intentions were still far in advance of anything the Liberal Party, including Gladstone, were ready to adopt as an Irish programme. He played little or no part in the contortions that produced the 1867 Reform Bill.

It was inevitable that Fortescue would be asked to return to the Irish Office in 1868. He was by far the ablest Irish Liberal in the House of Commons, and the only one fit for Cabinet rank. Ireland was at the centre of political debate, and the general situation there was still held to demand amenity, persuasion, and conciliation, such as only Fortescue could supply. Moreover, the fact that both the Lord-Lieutenant, Lord Spencer, and his Under-Secretary were new to their jobs, made it all the more necessary to retain a man with previous experience as Irish Secretary. But whether from reasons of salary, prestige, or more probably of personal interest, Fortescue had wanted the Colonial Office, and as early as 1868 felt hurt at not getting it.

During his two sessions as Irish Secretary, he suffered in reputation because the very importance of the legislation concerning Ireland led to his being by-passed or overruled. The Irish Church Act of 1869 and the Irish Land Act of 1870 were very much Gladstone's political property, so far as public appearances were concerned, while their preparation was to an unusual extent the work of the Cabinet and its committees, rather than of the responsible minister. Fortescue was only left with responsibility for the unenviable task of carrying the Peace Preservation Act (1870). In the case of the Land Bill, however, Fortescue was overruled rather than simply overshadowed.

In October 1869, Fortescue sketched a draft land bill, which, though representing average opinion in the Cabinet, was dismissed by Gladstone as too moderate.[1] Thereafter Fortescue's work was confined to drafting a bill on lines distinctly at variance with his own ideas, trying at times to tone down

[1] The account of the 1870 Land Bill given here is based on E. D. Steele's unpublished Cambridge Ph.D. thesis, 'Irish Land Reform and English Liberal Politics, 1865–70' (1963).

Gladstone's proposals but being put firmly in his place. Gladstone controlled the passage of the Bill through the Cabinet[1] as much as through Parliament, while Fortescue, it has been held, 'far from contributing to the success of the bill . . . seriously threatened it'.[2]

Fortescue's true part in the formation of Irish policy in 1869–70 was not known at the time. What is clear is that the fame went to Gladstone, while the setbacks rubbed off on him. In January 1871, after having himself pressed for a change of scene,[3] he found himself President of the Board of Trade, following Bright's retirement through ill health. He held this post till the ministry resigned in 1874, but his only notable contribution was to carry through a departmental bill which secured great advances in the safety of railway passengers. He did, however, continue to give loyal support to the general idea of the Government's Irish policy, as exemplified for instance in its ill-fated Irish University Bill of 1873.

The place of Lady Waldegrave[4] in his life is not easy to describe, least of all as it appeared to him. The bare facts are however fairly simple. He first met her in 1850, during her third marriage, and at once formed a virtuous attachment to her, a sentiment in which he was far from alone. Throughout the fifties, Lady Waldegrave held court to a circle of rising young men in the Peelite and Liberal ranks, without ever failing in her duty to her elderly husband. Fortescue waited, though far from certain of eventually winning her hand. In the end, her third husband, George Granville Harcourt, uncle of the politician, died on 19 December 1861. On 20 January 1863 she married Fortescue. Though none of her four marriages brought children, in 1860 she adopted Constance, her brother's daughter, who therefore became one of Fortescue's family and later the principal comfort of his old age.

Lady Waldegrave died suddenly, of a neglected minor infection, in 1879. Carlingford was thenceforward inconsolable,

[1] Ibid., p. 218.
[2] Ibid., p. 358.
[3] See below, appendix.
[4] See O. Wyndham Hewett, *Strawberry Fair: A Biography of Frances, Countess Waldegrave, 1821–1879* (London, 1956), and the article in the *Dictionary of National Biography*, written by Carlingford's friend Henry Grenfell.

the more so as he felt to blame, apparently for having allowed his wife not to take her illness seriously from the first. She left her husband a life interest in the Waldegrave estates, which she owned absolutely. Of these, Strawberry Hill was sold just after her death and Dudbrook, the large estate in Essex, was also sold just before Carlingford's death. The remaining estates, mostly at Chewton in Somerset, then reverted to the ninth Earl Waldegrave. Carlingford's natural melancholy and self-doubt were therefore augmented by the fact that he outlived her in a setting she had created, in houses which she had restored and enlarged, looking after estates which she had allowed to become encumbered with debt.

It may be useful simply to put down here what the reference books can tell us of Carlingford's estates as they were about 1885. Carlingford himself had only one small estate, and that, moreover, in Ireland, which he could truly call his own. This had been left to him by his father's sister and her husband, W. Ruxton, who died in 1865 and 1861 respectively. It was in his native county of Louth, where by far the largest estates were those of his brother, Lord Clermont. Listing these together with the Waldegrave inheritance, we find the resources of the family can be expressed as follows:

	acres	£ rent p.a.
Lord Carlingford: Estate in Louth, inherited from aunt	1,452	1,719
Estate in Carlow	686	583
Life interest in Waldegrave estates[1]	10,940	*c.* 12,000
Salary as Lord President of the Council		2,000
Lord Clermont: estates in Louth etc.	21,127	15,784

The apparent exactitude of these figures means very little, especially where Irish land is concerned, but they can only be stated as printed in contemporary works of reference. Their real interest lies in the fact that Carlingford was unable to live within his means. In his journal he states that he had spent, in 1884, much

---

[1] These consisted of 5,108 acres in Essex; 5,321 acres in Somerset; and 501 acres in Middlesex and E. Yorkshire.

more than his income. This was despite having a London residence
lent to him while in office, apparently free, by Northbrook, and
a substantial official salary to boot. This only brings out the depth
of the economic problems he was left to sort out after his wife's
death. He had to contend with poor relations and ne'er-do-wells
in his own family; with the need to find capital to develop his
collieries; with the fall in coal and corn prices; but above all, with
a crushing burden of debt on the estates. Living in the simplest
possible way and hardly entering society at all, he still needed,
when out of office, a large allowance from his brother to pay his
way. Only by such negative indications as this, and his estate at
death being only £4,000, can we discern the uphill struggle that
lay behind his apparent opulence.

However, perhaps neither his bereavement nor his financial
worries are as immediately relevant as background to the journal,
as is the fact that in 1884 the united pressure of most of his colleagues
had failed to make him resign from the Cabinet to make a place
for Rosebery. The episode epitomizes his standing so clearly and
has such important constitutional implications that it is worth
relating at length.

Carlingford's manner of life in the 1880's was bound to put
him on everyone's list of ministers 'who never would be missed'.[1]
While his colleagues strove fiercely for reputation, Carlingford
devoted himself to quiet reflection and poignant memories.
Largely by his own choice, he was more politically isolated and
personally detached than any other member of Gladstone's
second administration, except perhaps Selborne. In a cabinet
split by personal rivalries and jealousies he refused to take a
hand in the plotting that was almost continuously in progress,
and thereby placed himself in a dangerously exposed position.
His relations with his friend Northbrook were at this time
devoid of positive political content. In fact it was Granville,
and not his oldest political colleague, who seriously contested
Gladstone's right to bludgeon him into resignation in the autumn

---

[1] Phrase in *The Mikado* (1885), aimed at 'procrastinating politicians of a tem-
porising kind'.

of 1884. Even here, however, Granville at first entirely supported Gladstone's plans for replacing Carlingford with Rosebery, and it was not till a few weeks later that he called for the abandonment of the scheme, arguing that Carlingford's obstinacy left little room for manoeuvre and stressing the convenience of having in the Cabinet an Irishman who would assist the party in the upper house. Granville's lukewarm defence of Carlingford is therefore not to be seen as a demonstration of regard for a fellow Whig. It was clear, moreover, that Gladstone at no stage expected any minister to come forward in Carlingford's defence. Whatever help Carlingford eventually received from colleagues was based more on a technical view of the situation, than on general support for him as a person or Whig. Only the Queen believed that Carlingford added weight to the Cabinet, but although she promised to support him,[1] her advice does not seem to have been sought or given during the crisis.

Carlingford survived in 1884 above all because he peremptorily refused to discuss his departure. He would not yield an inch to Gladstone, because he had yielded to him so often before. Because he saw in his previous encounters with Gladstone the behaviour of a weak man, he was compelled in 1884 to be the worm that turned. His previous relations with Gladstone had been consistently unfortunate. Like other Whigs, he had lost ground when Gladstone became leader in the 1860s: he lost ground again when Gladstone resumed the leadership in 1880. His career needed a Liberal Party under Russell or Granville, if he were to achieve his main object between 1860 and 1880: the Colonial Secretaryship.[2] Instead, he was passed over in 1864 for Gladstone's friend Cardwell, and disappointed in 1868 and 1870 by being sent to Ireland and to the Board of Trade. On each of the occasions that Gladstone came between Carlingford and his ambitions, he dealt his blows without any adequate display of reluctance or ordinary consideration: he could not allow that Carlingford also was proud and thin-skinned, and in 1884 he had to pay for never having attempted to kindle amity.

[1] Carlingford to Clermont, 5 Dec. 1884; Carlingford papers.
[2] See appendix.

The events of 1880–1 have a particular relevance to Carlingford's obstinacy in 1884. It is difficult to place Carlingford in relation to the inner struggles of the Liberal leadership in 1874–80, though he clearly welcomed and supported Hartington's election in 1875. In the crucial year 1879–80, Carlingford was entirely *hors de combat* because of Lady Waldegrave's death. At the time of the general election, his views of his future were fluctuating and obscure, but inclined towards his leaving public life. While in this state, he was called back from Switzerland, where he was visiting a sick sister, by a letter from Granville pressing him to return and asking if he was available to take part again in public life. Carlingford allowed himself to feel this amounted to an offer of a Cabinet post, and returned hastily to England, only to wait disconsolately in a London hotel without being sent for while Gladstone formed his ministry. Gladstone finally offered him the Lord-Lieutenancy of Ireland, without Cabinet office, which Carlingford peremptorily declined,[1] without discussion of reasons. Granville then offered Carlingford the embassy at Constantinople, which he accepted after much hesitation. Carlingford fully believed he would be spending the next few years in the east, and was quite looking forward to it, when he was informed that the Cabinet had decided to appoint Goschen instead. Again, the circumstances of the case made it appear that Gladstone's was the hostile hand at work as in 1870. Ironically, however, both Gladstone and Granville[2] were under the impression that Carlingford had declined the offer. Thereafter, Carlingford's relations with Gladstone were exceptionally perfunctory: Gladstone's attempt to remove him in the autumn of 1884 brought them into closer contact than at any time since 1874. When Carlingford finally entered the Government as Lord Privy Seal in 1881, without any administrative responsibilities, he did so in spite of considerable misgivings and at Gladstone's insistence,[3] in order that

[1] Carlingford to Granville, 27 Apr. 1880: Gladstone Papers, B.M. Add. MS. 44123, ff. 89–90; Edward Hamilton's diary, B.M. Add. MS. 48630, f. 4.

[2] Granville to Gladstone, 29 Apr. 1880: Gladstone to Granville, 2 May 1880 in A. Ramm, *The Political Correspondence of Mr Gladstone and Lord Granville 1876–1886*, i (Oxford, 1962), 122–3.

[3] Carlingford to Gladstone, 8 Apr. 1881: Gladstone Papers, B.M. Add. MS.

Ireland might be represented in the Cabinet—a point which Gladstone completely brushed aside in 1884. Further, while Carlingford had no objection to making the unsalaried office of Privy Seal available for Rosebery in 1884, Gladstone rejected any such compromise and insisted that Carlingford should give up the Lord Presidency, a working office he had taken over from Spencer quite eagerly in 1883[1] and which well suited his academic tastes. Carlingford had entered the Cabinet to oblige Gladstone, for reasons of Gladstone's own invention; he had carried out his duties respectably; and he was now asked to disappear from the scene by giving up an office which he actually cared to have. Carlingford's memories, his main source of companionship, plainly suggested therefore that only 'an absolute & dry refusal'[2] could prevent a repetition of previous events. What Gladstone interpreted simply as resolute and unaccountable attachment to office must be seen in the context of Carlingford's belief that Gladstone was incapable of treating him with reasonable consideration.

Throughout his negotiations to oust Carlingford, Gladstone's insensitivity to the feelings of his greatly bereaved colleague, incapable of 'that hopefulness which a man ought to feel if he enters utterly new scenes of public and private life',[3] led him to present his case entirely in terms of the general political situation. In particular, Gladstone calculated that by replacing Carlingford with Rosebery (his fixed intention throughout)[4] he would significantly reduce the challenge which the government faced in

---

44123, ff. 96–7. Following the appointment, Spencer wrote '. . . I have handed over Irish questions to Carlingford, who knows much more than I do about Irish matters.' Spencer to Cowper, 24 May 1881, in Lady Cowper, *Memoir of Earl Cowper, K.G., by his Wife* (London, 1913), 505.

[1] Carlingford to Gladstone, n.d. [15 Mar. 1883]: Gladstone Papers, B.M. Add. MS. 44123, f. 145.

[2] Gladstone to Granville, 13 Sept. 1884 in Ramm, op. cit. ii. 253.

[3] Carlingford to Granville, 4 Sept. 1884: Granville MSS., P.R.O. 30/29/22A.

[4] A rather breathless letter from Lord Reay to Rosebery (10 Oct. 1884, Rosebery MSS.), to the effect that Granville (referred to as 'our enemy'!) proposed to retire to make room for Rosebery, need not be taken too seriously. Its only basis is Reay's unsupported testimony as to allegations, also unsupported by other evidence, made by E. Hamilton about Granville's intentions.

Scotland as a result of a nationalist campaign mounted by the *Scotsman* and actively encouraged by Rosebery since his resignation in 1883. Gladstone made it the crux of his first letter to Carlingford:

> Scotland has felt, if not a little resented, the lack of anyone else in the Cabinet who could be at all addicted to her special interests, since the Duke of Argyll quitted it; and it is of real importance, with reference to the possibility, I might say the likelihood, of a somewhat early dissolution, that we should take every means of keeping our phalanx complete, and, if we can of enlarging it. There is no doubt that we should improve the position here [in Scotland], without worsening it elsewhere, by bringing some Scotchman, whom Scotchmen know and love, into the Cabinet.[1]

In addition, by sacrificing Carlingford rather than anyone else Gladstone could make plain his determination to provide a legislative as well as an executive remedy for Scotland's most pressing grievance. Carlingford, by speaking out in the Lords on 30 June 1884 against the proposal to transfer responsibility for Scottish education to the projected Scottish secretary, presented an obstacle to the plan for devolution which brought its author, Harcourt, to the verge of resignation.[2] Although Gladstone could probably have induced Carlingford to resign at this juncture[3] by taking Harcourt's side, he failed to do so, probably because the Scottish Liberals were themselves divided on whether they wanted Home Rule in education, and also because the need to eject Carlingford was not yet powerfully present in his mind. The delay gave Rosebery's ally, Charles Cooper, editor of the *Scotsman*, a chance to whip up opposition to Carlingford: by the end of the year he had made a series of direct attacks and had 'more in pickle'.[4]

Rosebery's antagonism to Carlingford went back to 1881,

---

[1] Gladstone to Carlingford, 7 Sept. 1884: Carlingford C. 324, Somerset County Record Office.

[2] Harcourt to Gladstone, 28 June 1884: Gladstone Papers, B.M. Add. MS. 44199, ff. 48–53.

[3] Carlingford to Gladstone, 29 June & 1 July 1884: Gladstone Papers, B.M. Add. MS. 44123, ff. 215–18.

[4] Cooper to Rosebery, 2 Dec. 1884: Rosebery MSS., box 9.

when Argyll's resignation left the Privy Seal vacant and the Cabinet without a Scotsman: that this was the only source of Rosebery's animosity, is evident from the way the two men got on well together during their brief period as colleagues in 1885. But in the late summer of 1884, Rosebery and Harcourt, those nearest at hand when Gladstone was making up his mind, were exceptionally committed to treating Carlingford as someone who could and should be lightly brushed aside. It was their pressure, combined with his personal impressions of the situation in Scotland, that forced Gladstone into action.

During Gladstone's campaign in Midlothian, 28 August–1 September 1884, Rosebery was received in an 'extraordinary manner . . . though [the audiences] had assembled to listen to another and greater man'.[1] It was only then that Rosebery's promotion became an object of really pressing concern: thus the one positive result to emerge from the ensuing attempt to dismiss Carlingford was 'an absolute recognition of [Rosebery's] title to the Cabinet'.[2] In order to facilitate his entry, Gladstone in November 1884 abandoned his ideas about the size of a Cabinet which had previously led him to insist on creating a vacancy before bringing Rosebery in.

Scotland and Rosebery's promotion provided Gladstone with the means to defend his ruthless treatment of Carlingford. He also briefly mentioned the Reform crisis. At a later stage in the negotiations he made use of proposed rearrangements in the education department. These were the urgent, public problems for which Gladstone tried to persuade Carlingford to sacrifice himself. In some sense they affected Gladstone's conduct and judgement throughout by reinforcing his determination and overcoming his scruples. On the other hand, his ruthlessness, casuistry, and lack of tact all existed apart from the passing issues which justified them. Gladstone took the decision to browbeat Carlingford in the knowledge that arrangements for one resignation (that of Dodson) had already been satisfactorily completed,

[1] Edward Hamilton's diary, 30 Aug. 1884: Hamilton Papers, B.M. Add. MS. 48637, ff. 70–1.
[2] Edward Hamilton to Rosebery, 11 Oct. 1884: Rosebery MSS., box 25.

before he left to stay with Rosebery at Dalmeny. As he presented
it to Granville, Gladstone's subsequent action against Carlingford
followed from the conviction that two resignations were better
than one.

There is however a sub-plot at the level of administrative reform,
which must be referred to here in parenthesis, though it played
little visible part in discussion in autumn 1884. Gladstone had long
held strong views in favour of turning the honorific ministerial
offices either into functional ministries, or into unpaid nominal
posts. In his second ministry, these ideas came to a head. The
Privy Seal became unpaid in 1883, and the Chancellor of the
Duchy became in effect responsible for agriculture in that year.
Stripped of agriculture, at least at day-to-day level, the Lord
President was left with education: but the Scottish Secretaryship
Bill threatened to remove one part of that from his grasp, while
Childers' committee of 1884 on educational administration reported in favour of the entire separation of education from the
Privy Council. It was, therefore, the long-term policy of the
government—which in this context meant Gladstone and Childers
—to remove the main functions of the Lord Presidency till it
became a mere unpaid title of honour to be held along with a
working office. In fact it is impossible to know how committed
Gladstone and Childers were to this reorganization: if in the
longer term the Lord Presidency was itself marked for the axe,
this had no real bearing on the manoeuvre of autumn 1884, which
was directed against Carlingford as a person and not against his
office, which Rosebery was meant to inherit unimpaired.

The indirect cause of the abortive attempt to dismiss Carlingford was Trevelyan's failure as Irish Secretary. The latter's self-
acknowledged incapacity to manage Irish business in the Commons
made his replacement a matter for serious discussion at the end
of July 1884.[1] Spencer suggested that Trevelyan and Lefevre,
First Commissioner of Works, should simply change places.[2] But
such an obvious solution was effectively undermined by the need
(acknowledged by all those concerned) to promote Trevelyan to

[1] Trevelyan to Gladstone, 26 July 1884: Gladstone Papers, B.M. Add. MS. 44335.
[2] Edward Hamilton's Diary, 25 July 1884: B.M. Add. MS. 48637, f. 30.

the Cabinet at the time of transferring him. No one thought Lefevre could be induced to accept the Irish Secretaryship while his successor as First Commissioner held that office on more advantageous terms then he had done. In view of Gladstone's aversion to an enlarged Cabinet, rearrangements at the Irish Office depended entirely therefore on a resignation from among its existing members. From the beginning only Dodson, Chancellor of the Duchy, was mentioned. During a conversation in the previous April with Gladstone, he had asked for a peerage in the event of a dissolution because he expected to lose his seat at the ensuing election.[1] Ultimately, the plan adopted in order to remove Dodson depended largely on the presence of such a fear in his mind. But by failing to send a letter embodying his request, Dodson left Gladstone inadequately prepared to take action against him. At the end of July only Edward Hamilton, Gladstone's secretary, suggested that Dodson's resignation should be made a precondition of his immediate elevation.[2]

The opportunity to get rid of Dodson finally appeared in mid-August 1884, when at Gladstone's prompting he committed himself on paper with a request 'to be advanced to the Upper House at the close of the present Parliament'.[3] Gladstone sent the letter on to Granville with the comment that 'here was the power of vacating a Commons seat'.[4] Dodson's eventual disappearance followed quite easily from this deduction, despite occasional flashes of resentment at the unflattering terms he was offered.[5] Unlike Carlingford, he obliged Gladstone by fitting in with the arrangements proposed for his removal. He survived until October, not on account of his own recalcitrance, but because the possibility of simultaneously announcing two resignations had occurred.

A few days before Dodson sent his letter, Granville had reminded

[1] Dodson to Gladstone, 19 Aug. 1884: Gladstone Papers, B.M. Add. MS. 44252, ff. 234–5.

[2] Edward Hamilton's Diary, 25 July 1884: loc. cit.

[3] Dodson to Gladstone, 19 Aug. 1884: loc. cit.

[4] Gladstone to Granville, 29 Aug. 1884 in A. Ramm, op. cit. ii. 239.

[5] Spencer to Granville, 11 Oct. 1884: Granville MSS., P.R.O. 30/29/29A.

Gladstone of the need to fill up the embassy at Constantinople, vacant since Dufferin's appointment as Viceroy of India, and suggested Carlingford as one among ten possible candidates.[1] In reply Gladstone singled out Carlingford on the grounds that he had 'the advantages of a very equitable mind'.[2] The subsequent manoeuvres effectually obscured the fact that Carlingford had any qualification other than a Cabinet seat marked for redistribution. Originally Gladstone may well have regarded Carlingford as the right man for the job. But in the interval between Gladstone's selection of Carlingford for the Constantinople embassy on 16 August and Granville's first approach to him on 3 September,[3] Dodson's letter had arrived and the decision to remove him had been taken by Gladstone and Granville. These events completely altered the light in which Gladstone was considering the question of Carlingford's removal. With one resignation virtually settled, Carlingford's replacement acquired an urgency bordering on indispensability. Together they offered 'a possibility of manipulation'[4] that could not be associated with merely one Cabinet change. Within six days of receiving Dodson's letter, Gladstone had decided on a plan[5] which until November 1884 he refused to modify in face of Carlingford's resistance on the one hand and alternative proposals put forward by senior colleagues on the other. Carlingford was to go to Constantinople,[6] Dodson to the Lords, and Rosebery and Trevelyan were to replace them. Briefly, towards the end of September after Carlingford had met him 'at every point with a hard and resolute negative',[7] Gladstone did consider a modification—admitting Rosebery to the Cabinet as First Commissioner[8] or Privy Seal until the Scottish Secretary

[1] Granville to Gladstone, 15 Aug. 1884, in A. Ramm, op. cit. ii. 227.

[2] Gladstone to Granville, 16 Aug. 1884, in A. Ramm, op. cit. ii. 229.

[3] Granville to Carlingford (copy), 3 Sept. 1884: Granville MSS., P.R.O. 30/29/28A.

[4] Gladstone to Granville, 24 Aug. 1884, in A. Ramm, op. cit. ii. 234.

[5] Henry Seymour (a secretary of Gladstone's) to Edward Hamilton, 26 Aug. 1884: Hamilton Papers, B.M. Add. MS. 48615, unfoliated.

[6] Although he was offered the Berlin embassy as an alternative it was never intended that he should have it.

[7] Gladstone to Granville, 19 Sept. 1884, in A. Ramm, op. cit. ii. 260.

[8] Edward Hamilton's diary, 24 Sept. 1884: B.M. Add. MS. 48637, f. 91.

Bill passed,[1] without dismissing Carlingford—but only with the intention of emphasizing the superiority of his original plan, and by early October he had returned to it. Dodson therefore was left in suspense for nearly two months (and was clearly expecting a further postponement even then[2]) in the hope of obtaining grounds for a public claim, to accompany the admission of two recruits to the Cabinet, that the Government had been materially reconstructed.

With a fairly rigid plan clearly formulated, Gladstone took over from Granville and moved directly against Carlingford. His fixed determination, however, was not accompanied by the tactical ingenuity necessary to carry it into effect. To a large extent this was due to a conviction that Carlingford had no other defensible course open to him, except acquiescence in the part Gladstone had prepared. In face of Granville's protests about the hounding of 'a popular man [and] the only Irishman in the Cabinet',[3] Gladstone excused his 'rough and butchering business' in the belief that 'our case is strong and the thing just'.[4] A heavy, oppressive tone and a formal manner lacking in subtlety both reflected Gladstone's view that a blank refusal of the type Carlingford actually returned was virtually inconceivable. Yet Edward Hamilton,[5] like Granville, had strong doubts from the beginning about whether Carlingford could ever be induced to fall in with Gladstone's request. The miscalculations that occurred therefore owed more to Gladstone's prejudices than to the advice of those closest to him throughout the crisis.

The actual conduct of the negotiations made it easy for Carlingford to resist instead of underlining the absence of any alternative except resignation. Apart from dispersing Carlingford's goodwill, Gladstone's attitude contrasted so strongly with Granville's

[1] Gladstone to Lord Richard Grosvenor (copy), 27 Sept. 1884: Gladstone Papers, B.M. Add. MS. 44547, ff. 114-15.

[2] Gladstone to Dodson (copy), 15 Oct. 1884: B.M. Add. MS. 44252, f. 236.

[3] Granville to Gladstone, 11 Sept. 1884, in A. Ramm, op. cit. ii. 253.

[4] Gladstone to Granville, 9 Sept. 1884, in A. Ramm, op. cit. ii. 251.

[5] Edward Hamilton's diary, 11 & 13 Sept. 1884: B.M. Add. MS. 48637, ff. 77-8.

that Carlingford had only to refer to the discrepancy in order to produce an effective rejoinder. Whereas Granville had laid emphasis on Carlingford's suitability in the belief that he 'would make a good Ambassador'[1] and mentioned 'the deterrent appearance of home political prospects'[2] only as an additional inducement, Gladstone dealt summarily with any intrinsic claims Carlingford had to the post before passing on to describe the situation in Scotland. Carlingford replied: '. . . your letter is not an offer of an embassy, as his [Granville's] was, but a very urgent request that I sh[ould] take it, for the purpose of leaving my office and seat in the Cabinet for an influential and distinguished Scotch peer.'[3] Whether or not Carlingford inferred the disagreement between Granville and Gladstone over the tactics to be adopted from the terms of their letters, his exploitation of it could scarcely have been more successful.

After Carlingford had explained his position so unequivocally in his letter of 11 September, Gladstone was reduced to verbal skirmishing about the conditions on which Carlingford had accepted the privy seal in 1881—whether on 'the old and regular footing'[4] (as Gladstone claimed) or with 'charge of Irish business in the H[ouse] of Lords'[5] (as Carlingford claimed)—in an attempt to get Carlingford to admit that he would be prepared to hold 'a seat in the Cabinet without specific office'.[6] The concession however was more apparent than real since Carlingford's ability to remain as Lord Privy Seal effectively depended upon his position as Lord President. In 1883 the Privy Seal had been permanently deprived of a salary, despite Carlingford's protests,[7] as a first step towards its extinction. Gladstone's attempt to confine

---

[1] Granville to Spencer, 16 Sept. 1884: Spencer MSS.

[2] Granville to Carlingford (copy), 3 Sept. 1884: Granville MSS., P.R.O. 30/29/28A.

[3] Carlingford to Gladstone, 11 Sept. 1884: B.M. Add. MS. 44123, f. 226.

[4] Gladstone to Carlingford (copy), 16 Sept. 1884: B.M. Add. MS. 44123, f. 232.

[5] Carlingford to Gladstone, 11 Sept. 1884: loc. cit.

[6] Gladstone to Carlingford (copy), 11 Sept. 1884: Gladstone Papers, B.M. Add. MS. 44123, f. 229. Gladstone to Granville, 13 Sept. 1884, in A. Ramm, op. cit., ii. 253–4.

[7] Carlingford to Gladstone, 29 May and 19 July 1883: B.M. Add. MS. 44123, ff. 171 & 186. When the Conservative government was formed in June 1885,

Carlingford to the Privy Seal alone, therefore, was designed to enhance the attractions of Constantinople by destroying the possibility of a financially secure place for him within the Cabinet. But Carlingford struck back vigorously at this point with the suggestion that Gladstone should bear his own manner of entry into the Cabinet in mind and bring Rosebery in as Privy Seal.[1]

In mid-September Gladstone shifted his attention from the Privy Seal to the Lord Presidency and the final phase of his direct negotiations with Carlingford consisted largely of a threatened attack on Carlingford's departmental responsibilities. Childers in reminding Gladstone[2] of a report drawn up by a select committee on education[3] provided him with sound, administrative justification. The report recommended the creation of a separate board of education with its own representative in the Cabinet: by carrying it into effect Gladstone could convert the Lord Presidency, whose weight derived from its connection with the education department, into as nominal an office as the Privy Seal. He sent a copy of the report to Carlingford calculating that it would induce 'a well judging man to resign'[4]; but Carlingford returned it without comment.[5] The failure to get a response led Gladstone to conclude that Carlingford was 'ready to submit to the stripping off of the weightiest of the functions now in his hands'[6] and in early October the whole proposal was dropped for the time being. Indeed, Gladstone seems to have been struck by it only insofar as it provided him with an additional weapon to use against Carlingford at a time when his previous ammunition had been uselessly expended.[7] In replying to Childers's reminder, he expressly linked

Harrowby, the new incumbent, found that he could not even get an allowance to cover the running expenses of the office: Northcote's diary, 26 June 1885: Iddesleigh Papers, B.M. Add. MS. 50063A, f. 435.
[1] Carlingford to Gladstone, 15 Sept. 1884: B.M. Add. MS. 44123, ff. 230–1.
[2] Childers to Gladstone, 16 Sept. 1884: B.M. Add. MS. 44311, ff. 138–9.
[3] It is dated 31 July 1884: B.M. Add. MS. 44123, f. 222.
[4] Gladstone to Granville, 23 Sept. 1884, in A. Ramm, op. cit. ii. 264–5.
[5] Gladstone to Granville, 20 Sept. 1884, in A. Ramm, op. cit. ii. 262.
[6] Gladstone to Rosebery, 10 Oct. 1884: Rosebery MSS., box 18.
[7] Edward Hamilton's diary, 24 Sept. 1884: B.M. Add. MS. 48637, f. 91.

3

his interest in the report with his conviction that 'something ought to be done for a leading Scotchman'.[1] Yet despite the readiness with which Gladstone concluded at this stage that Carlingford could be turned into a figurehead without being brought to the point of resignation, Carlingford probably did regard the projected ministry of education as potentially the most serious threat to his position. In February 1885 Childers, at Gladstone's request, mentioned to Carlingford that the report was about to be implemented.[2] As a result Carlingford took the offensive by sending a long letter to Gladstone which bluntly restated all his well-known objections to the proposal.[3]

At the end of September 1884 Gladstone sent all his correspondence with Carlingford to the Liberal chief whip, Lord Richard Grosvenor[4] in order that the crisis could become a matter of joint discussion among selected members of the Cabinet. Until that date it had been the concern only of the individual ministers whom Gladstone had chosen to consult. When the Cabinet reassembled in London early in October to prepare the Government's programme for the coming session, an informal meeting attended by Grosvenor, Granville, Spencer, Harcourt, Childers, and Gladstone was held on 7 October 1884 to consider the whole question of ministerial rearrangements.[5] All the commoners present agreed that Rosebery and Carlingford could not both be allowed seats in the Cabinet. Granville and Spencer probably stood by Carlingford's right to remain, for 'a great fight'[6] took place between them and the commoners. Evidently they both capitulated in the end, since later in the day they called on Carlingford in a final effort to persuade him to go to Constan-

---

[1] Gladstone to Childers (copy), 20 Sept. 1884: B.M. Add. MS. 44547, f. 111.

[2] Carlingford to Spencer, 10 Feb. 1885: Spencer MSS.

[3] Carlingford to Gladstone, 21 Feb. 1885: Gladstone Papers, B.M. Add. MS. 44123, ff. 241–4.

[4] Gladstone to Grosvenor (copy), 27 Sept. 1884: Gladstone Papers, B.M. Add. MS. 44547, ff. 114–15.

[5] Edward Hamilton's diary, 7 Oct. 1884: B.M. Add. MS. 48637, ff. 116–17. Granville to Hartington, 7 Oct. 1884: Devonshire MSS. 340/1546.

[6] Granville to Hartington, ibid.

tinople. According to the account Spencer gave Rosebery,[1] Granville began by saying, 'Now will you let me talk to you as I should to my brother Freddy in such a case'[2] and then gave a fairly clear hint that only by resignation could he forestall dismissal, before concluding with the advice 'that to allow myself to be turned out would be an impossible attitude'.[3] Carlingford replied by flatly refusing to reconsider his position and impressed Granville by making out 'a good case'[4] for himself in terms of public duty and the personal hardship[5] involved in resigning. The next day he put the matter beyond doubt with a letter to Granville in which he directly challenged the propriety of the remarks made about the possibility of dismissal.[6]

The same group of ministers met again the following day[7] after a Cabinet to hear reports from Granville and Spencer. It was generally agreed that 'no amount of pressure and strong hints' would have any effect, and Gladstone was left to decide whether 'to carry out the fight to the bitter end'.[8] The rapidity with which he drew back at this point, besides showing that Spencer and Granville had been sent with only idle threats, makes it doubtful whether Gladstone seriously considered the possibility of dismissing Carlingford in the full technical sense at any stage. His one source of advice on this general issue, Harcourt, merely

[1] Rosebery's diary, 13 Oct. 1884, quoted in R. R. James, *Rosebery* (London, 1963), 160.

[2] Curiously, Granville had used this same phrase when persuading Carlingford not to resign in 1870: see appendix.

[3] Carlingford to Clermont, 11 Oct. 1884: Strachie MSS., Strachie: Carlingford Papers, Somerset County Record Office.

[4] Granville to Hartington, 7 Oct. 1884: Devonshire MSS. 340/1546.

[5] In the year 1884 Carlingford spent much more than his total income, even taking into account his official salary. Not until 1885 did he have an arrangement with his brother for an increased allowance should he lose office: and there was no real likelihood in 1884 that he would accept a lucrative post overseas. His financial prospects on loss of office were therefore dismal, yet he nevertheless showed himself willing to resign over Scottish education in 1884 and over several issues in 1885. It was quite clearly not loss of office, but extrusion from office, which he was determined not to contemplate.

[6] Carlingford to Granville, 8 Oct. 1884: Granville MSS., P.R.O. 30/29/29A.

[7] Edward Hamilton's diary, 8 Oct. 1884: B.M. Add. MS. 48637, ff. 120-1.

[8] Edward Hamilton's diary, 8 Oct. 1884: B.M. Add. M.S. 48637, ff. 120-1

provided personal, dogmatic opinions, dressed up as constitutional law, to the effect that 'the Prime Minister had the same authority to modify the [Cabinet] as he has to construct it'.[1] Gladstone was influenced more powerfully by the absence of any precedent in his own direct experience which could justify 'a measure of the severest nature' in circumstances that were 'not favourable'.[2] He therefore went no further than to claim that 'for a great public object & without circumstances of disparagement, it may be the duty of a Prime Minister in rare circumstances to suggest to a colleague the propriety of his withdrawal.'[3]

Gladstone's letter of 10 October to Rosebery[4] summarizing the attempts made to remove Carlingford, as an explanation of the delay in bringing him into the Cabinet, marked the final abandonment of Gladstone's original plan for the Government's reconstruction. Thus, there ceased to be any point in holding back Dodson's resignation, and Trevelyan succeeded him on 18 October 1884. The problem of Rosebery came forward again for consideration shortly afterwards on the death of Henry Fawcett, the Postmaster-General,[5] on 6 November. Gladstone seized on it as an excuse to throw overboard the carefully guarded rules which had dictated his conduct throughout the crisis over Carlingford. By proposing that Lefevre, Fawcett's successor, should hold office with a seat in the Cabinet, he was able to claim that the existing balance between peers and commoners could only be preserved through an enlarged membership by the simultaneous inclusion of Rosebery as First Commissioner.[6] In an exactly parallel manner, Gladstone could have ended the crisis over

---

[1] Harcourt to Gladstone, 22 Sept. 1884: Gladstone Papers, B.M. Add. MS. 44199, f. 89.
[2] Gladstone to Harcourt (copy), 25 Sept. 1884: Gladstone Papers, B.M. Add. MS. 44547, f. 114.   [3] Ibid.
[4] Gladstone to Rosebery, 10 Oct. 1884: Rosebery MSS. box 18.
[5] Fawcett's death was quite unexpected. It is just possible that he was being considered for promotion to the Cabinet to balance the admission of Rosebery. Fawcett's biographer, Leslie Stephen, writing under some constraint, hinted at some such prospect, but seemed also to deny it by an altogether more definite statement that Fawcett would have resigned, as Courtney did, over proportional representation.
[6] Edward Hamilton's diary, 8 Nov. 1884: B.M. Add. MS. 48638, ff. 40–1.

Carlingford at any time during its progress. On this occasion, Rosebery himself upset Gladstone's arrangements by refusing the office proposed to him,[1] nominally because of disagreement with the Government's Egyptian policy, but basically out of contempt for the office itself which had 'neither dignity nor importance'.[2] Despite the pressure put on him by Granville and Hartington[3] at Gladstone's request, Rosebery stood by his decision until February 1885, and then sacrificed his objections only as a patriotic gesture after the fall of Khartoum.

On Rosebery's admission to the Cabinet Carlingford gave up the Privy Seal—the solution he himself had recommended in the previous autumn. Further schemes, similar to this insofar as they entailed altering the Cabinet's existing equilibrium, had been canvassed by Spencer and Granville even at the time Gladstone was relying on them to induce Carlingford to resign. Spencer wanted Trevelyan's successor as Irish Secretary to have a seat in the Cabinet and saw an easy way to bring this about, by leaving Carlingford where he was to keep the balance between peers and commoners in the Cabinet, when Rosebery and the new Irish Secretary were promoted.[4] Granville endorsed this suggestion because he required alternatives to Gladstone after opposing the idea of a campaign to 'squeeze out' Carlingford.[5] As far as Carlingford was concerned these alternative plans amounted to valuable support in strategically decisive places. On 7 October when Spencer and Granville called with their threats of dismissal, they succeeded in leaving Carlingford with the clear impression that they thought Rosebery 'might be brought in without disturbing me, and had been arguing against Mr. G., who held that the difficulty of adding another peer to the Cabinet

[1] Rosebery to Gladstone, 11 Nov. 1884: Gladstone Papers, B.M. Add. MS. 44288, ff. 214–15.

[2] Rosebery to Granville (copy), 12 Nov. 1884: Rosebery MSS., box 60.

[3] Ibid. Hartington to Rosebery (copy), 27 Dec. 1884: Devonshire MSS. 340/1594. Rosebery to Hartington, 30 Dec. 1884: Devonshire MSS. 340/1595.

[4] Spencer to Gladstone, 20 Sept. 1884: Gladstone Papers, B.M. Add. MS. 44311, ff. 197–200.

[5] Granville to Spencer, 16 Sept. 1884: Spencer MSS., and Granville to Gladstone 11 Sept. 1884, in A. Ramm, op. cit. ii. 252–3.

would be insuperable'.[1] Only Harcourt, of the colleagues who
were in Gladstone's confidence throughout,[2] entirely supported
the way in which Gladstone sought to create an impression of
ministerial reconstruction without altering the size of the Cabinet.
Harcourt's agreement however arose, not from any real belief in
Gladstone's ideas about the appropriate size and internal balance
of the Cabinet, but because his proposals for the general reconstruction of the Liberal leadership, in or out of office, made
it necessary for him to win Gladstone's confidence. Of the other
ministers who were brought in during September and attended
the meeting on 7 October, Childers wanted Carlingford's
removal only in an incidental and administrative connexion, as a
preliminary step towards the creation of a ministry of education,
and Grosvenor's only task was to carry out whatever decision
might be arrived at. Gladstone's attempt to make Carlingford's
position a question of the collective power of the Cabinet over its
membership failed, therefore, out of a lack of unanimity. With
Spencer and Granville emerging openly on Carlingford's side,
any further efforts to bring ministerial pressure to bear could have
split the Cabinet between commoners and peers. Thus Gladstone's
only alternative to raising issues that involved the possible
resignation of the Government was to drop the whole matter. In
a Cabinet where reputations were guarded so closely, any dis-
turbance of a precariously balanced equilibrium set everybody
(except Carlingford) thinking how he could turn it to his own
advantage. The chances of successfully removing Carlingford
without bringing up these matters of fundamental concern
depended on Carlingford's amenability in August and September.
Any prolonged controversy on almost any subject at this time
inevitably raised the question what kind of party the Liberal Party
wanted to be. In autumn 1884 no one yet wanted a test of strength
on that question. The Carlingford case therefore focused on the
immediate constitutional issue of prime ministerial power to
induce resignation, and could not safely pass beyond it. It is for

[1] Carlingford to Clermont, 11 Oct. 1884: Carlingford Papers.
[2] The radical ministers, Chamberlain and Dilke, appear to have played no part
in the episode at any point.

that reason that it is a *locus classicus* for Victorian constitutional doctrine and practice.

Carlingford survived his long period of persecution. However, the bitterly fought struggle had made it abundantly clear to all his colleagues that his final departure from the Liberal leadership could not be long delayed. Carlingford himself realized that he had ceased to count. A lesser man would have revealed his mortification by passing hostile judgements on his colleagues in the privacy of his journal. Yet, because of his generous and compassionate nature he was saved from falling into pettiness. Where Carlingford does hold a low opinion of any individual (Harcourt being the most obvious case) his views are conclusively borne out by other evidence. By contrast, the dominant members of the Cabinet were so consumed by jealousy that they were completely incapable of appreciating each other. Thus Carlingford's almost complete detachment from the events he records enhances rather than detracts from his virtues as a diarist.

When Carlingford started his journal at the beginning of 1885, politicians were getting their breath back after a period of total absorption in the constitutional crisis over the third Reform Bill. There was general agreement that the new franchise had created a quite new political situation, but there was also a general feeling that there need be no rush to strike out any new line. In part this simply turned on the fact that most of the coming year would be occupied with the mechanics of passing the Reform Bill, even though this had ceased to involve major controversy. With little prospect of the expected new situation crystallizing before a new register of electors could be created in the autumn, the only attempts to break new ground were those made by Goschen and Chamberlain, and their campaigns inevitably appeared premature. Chamberlain's January campaign for a new radicalism, for instance, failed to win support from Dilke and other radicals, just as Goschen's campaign for a new party of broadly-based reaction remained an isolated effort not backed by the Liberal moderates who really mattered.

Moreover Gladstone was not attempting to initiate a new

departure in Irish affairs, at least until two other ministers, Spencer and Chamberlain, acting outside the context of public campaigning, made it the question of the moment at the end of April. Spencer indeed would have appreciated Cabinet consideration of his programme of Irish reforms, at any time from January 1885 onwards. Chamberlain, who in January had hoped to work out an arrangement for increasing Irish autonomy, largely let the matter drop in February and March, and when his interest revived in April the idea of using Irish policy to force a decisive conflict with Spencer and the Whigs initially played no part in his calculations. The greatest obstruction to an early and constructive approach to Irish policy was the fact that Gladstone exercised his control over the Cabinet agenda to prevent any discussion till 28 April. It was only after an unforeseen deadlock had emerged in Cabinet that Gladstone showed signs of passionate concern about finding the right Liberal policy for Ireland.

The general understanding that the time had not come to go deeply into Irish, domestic and party matters meant that by default interest in Cabinet centred on a fortuitous succession of foreign crises and on plans, of which Carlingford knew nothing, for reconstructing the Liberal ministry for purposes of gratifying individual ambitions. In fact, the reason the crises over foreign affairs cut so deeply was not due to depth of feeling over the often minor questions at issue but to hopes that a bitter enough conflict in the Cabinet might set off a desired series of promotions and retirements. Ministers were curiously sure that the future held a long succession of Liberal governments, and so the key question was their relevant positions inside them. In particular Harcourt and Dilke had especially clear ideas of the kind of promotion that was their due at the first upheaval, while Derby, Childers and Carlingford were expected to be dropped as soon as possible. A much larger but attractive possibility to most ministers was that of Hartington replacing Gladstone, a development which Chamberlain and Dilke privately regarded as highly desirable. Thus Cabinet divisions invariably had more than one meaning.

There were three major crises over foreign affairs in 1885. Throughout January the Cabinet was wholly absorbed in negotiations with France and other powers over Egyptian finance. The range of choices here was so wide and the details so difficult that the Cabinet did not expect to reach any agreed solution such as was surprisingly and silently reached at the beginning of February, when a new understanding with France put the Egyptian question into cold storage for the medium future. By 4 February it was clear that the Liberal Party, by pure good fortune, need not try to reach any collective view as to what should be done about Egypt in the long-term, to the immense relief of everyone.

Up to this point ministers had regarded the British campaign in the Sudan with optimism or complacency. The progress of Wolseley's Nile expedition had hardly been discussed in Cabinet at all. The only time ministers were called upon to decide about military plans in January was at a Cabinet on the 7th when they authorized a second smaller expedition to be sent to the port of Suakin.[1] Thus the news received on 5 February of the fall of Khartoum involved quite major adjustments in attitudes. The question was seen as one of prestige. This was so both in the initial phase when the Cabinet embarked on a potentially un-limited commitment to reconquest and in March and April when the problem was to find ways of reversing earlier plans without apparent loss of honour. On a political level the fall of Khartoum produced two results which nullified each other. On the one hand Hartington's stock rose and renewed attempts were made to form a 'patriotic government' under him, a development which Chamberlain was anxious to promote. On the other hand the disaster in the Sudan gave Gladstone a new lease of life. The well-founded assumption, which had been prevalent in January, that he might retire from old age and ill health, vanished overnight and was only revived thereafter by Gladstone himself as a way of bringing his colleagues to heel.

The third crisis in foreign affairs was probably caused by British involvement in the Sudan. Russian activities in Central Asia had been viewed with great apprehension since the Merv crisis in the previous year, but it was only after the Government had

[1] Hartington was given discretion to take positive action, 7 Jan., and within two days decided to do nothing.

announced its plans for major operations on the Nile that Russian policy seriously began to alarm ministers in general. A clash between the Russian and Afghan forces at Penjdeh on 30 March created a situation in which an early outbreak of war seemed highly likely. In retrospect the distinctive feature of the crisis is the bellicosity shown by the former opponents of Disraeli's Eastern policy of 1876–80 rather than the shrewd diplomacy by which they averted calamity.

When Russian difficulties became less acute at the end of April there was henceforth in fact if not in name only one set of questions concerning the Cabinet. These were what decisions to take about the character of the Liberal Party and its place in the general party structure, in order to fight the general election and to create the basis for a subsequent Liberal government. The answers to these questions were not really settled till the Conservatives declared for coercion in January 1886. The manoeuvres in the interval were unproductive, protracted, and bitter to a degree. The activities of the Liberal Cabinet in May and June therefore belong less to the history of Cabinet administration than to the history of party structure. One obvious result of this sharp change in the character of Liberal policy was that there ceased to be much scope for a Cabinet diarist such as Carlingford.

The final years of Carlingford's life are difficult to construe. The problem is whether any single explanation can be given of his sudden plunge into retirement. Clearly ill health and general ennui temporarily gained the upper hand over him in 1886, and perhaps for years beyond that.[1] Clearly he was far too decided a supporter of the Union to maintain even the most attenuated links with the Gladstone ministry of 1886. Moreover, irrespective of Home Rule, he had in any case been marked out as superfluous so far as membership of the Cabinet was concerned. Yet none of these points quite covers the demise of his public identity in 1886. His illness, for instance, did not prevent him from remaining Lord-

---

[1] For indications of continuing poor health, see Carlingford to Gladstone, 18 May 1886, refusing an invitation to the Queen's birthday dinner on health grounds: B.M. Add. MS. 44788, f. 119; a notice in *The Times*, 2 Aug. 1886; and Carlingford to Selborne, 15 Sept. 1888: Selborne MSS. 1871, f. 112.

Lieutenant of Essex till 1892, or from taking on the presidency of the Somerset Liberal Unionist Association: the Home Rule split could have meant the beginning of a new career as the Liberal Unionists' authority on Irish affairs; and he might, despite the general view that he should be dropped, have gained important office in February 1886, had it not been for Home Rule.

During 1885 the shadows were drawing in upon Carlingford. He handled no important business. The educational responsibilities of his department appeared to be about to be removed and placed in other hands, despite his serious and well-founded protests. He was not called upon by Spencer or Gladstone to deliberate upon the formation of Irish policy. Spencer's Irish reform programme of 1885 was probably unknown to Carlingford, till he received a belated explanation in an unforeseen conversation with the Viceroy. As far as Gladstone went, Carlingford did not exist. Their only private conversation in 1885 was on the train to Windsor when they resigned (24 June). Carlingford's last serious correspondence with Gladstone was a letter of 21 February 1885 to him on the proposed reorganization of education, a departmental question of a kind which necessarily had to be referred to the Prime Minister. Otherwise it is clear that from the beginning of 1885 there was no question of Gladstone and Carlingford consulting or even chatting together unless circumstances forced it on them. Even when Rosebery was brought into the Cabinet, thus removing the supposedly urgent need to drop Carlingford, Gladstone's remoteness did not change: he simply had no use for Carlingford. Gladstone and Carlingford did not communicate between June 1885 and February 1886. Gladstone's talk with Carlingford on the train on 24 June was possibly the last between the two men.

Thus, irrespective of Home Rule, Carlingford's chances of re-entering the Liberal leadership were already slim or non-existent by June 1885. He himself was fully aware of this, yet it is not clear what conclusions he drew as to his future path. Was his last speech in the House of Lords, on 21 July 1885, intended as a last speech? Was his fairly vigorous election campaign in Somerset in autumn 1885 intended to keep him in the front ranks of the party, or did he act chiefly with a view to aiding his son-in-law's candidacy and maintaining his own local position against the new Liberalism of the unauthorized programme? There are few clues in the diary or elsewhere as to his aims at this time, for all his activities brought home to him afresh the sadness of the contrast between time present and time past, and this occupied his thoughts more than anything else. What is more probable is that his departure abroad on 21 November 1885 was a deliberate act of political withdrawal designed to shield him from any mortification that a coming change of ministry might involve.

It was only while abroad that he discovered an opportunity to leave politics, not because of his failure as a politician, but because of the firmness of his Unionist principles. Not only were his opinions on Home Rule entirely consistent at all stages of the controversy, but they could only enhance the terms on which he made his inevitable withdrawal. The mere fact of his being abroad contributed to his Unionism, since it insulated him from the growing sense of inevitability which bore many Unionists towards Gladstone in December 1885–January 1886, as the Conservatives eliminated themselves from playing the role of a realistic party of government in relation to existing Irish circumstances.

Carlingford was abroad from 21 November 1885 to 12 February 1886—the whole initial phase of the crisis. Despite some fairly severe fever which seems to have precipitated a much more long-drawn-out nervous breakdown, he emerged in this period as probably the most committed advocate of unqualified resistance among the Liberal ex-Cabinet. On 31 December he wrote to Northbrook and 'told him I was decidedly for resistance to any Home Rule plan': on 8 January he wrote to Trevelyan, arguing the case against Home Rule 'à propos of a speech he made the other day'. Neither letter can now be traced, and for a fuller statement of his position one must turn to his letters to his Irish landlord brother, Lord Clermont:

My only political correspondents at this moment are Northbrook and H. Grenfell. I have told them both that I am for resistance to the creation of any elected body, under any name or limitations, in Dublin.

That once done, where shall we stop? The policy of absolute refusal will be very difficult, and may have formidable consequences: it *may* prove impossible but I do not despair, and in any case, I sh. resist. I hope it may be possible to keep Ld. Salisbury in for the present.[1]

Later Carlingford added some afterthoughts:

I don't think it is at all likely that I shall be in office, so as to earn £2000 a year, as I did for four years. Even if Gladstone were to offer me office again, it does not look as if I could accept, considering his probable Irish policy. I quite agree with you about the scheme of a central council in Dublin. I opposed it when I first heard it mooted before we went out of office. . . I should not wonder if it proved to be the plan which [Gladstone] now has in his head.[2]

Ireland, Carlingford thought, was 'not a nation' and any national government would be merely the National League—'a mass of peasants manipulated by a few'.[3] On 3 February, having heard nothing from London, Carlingford explained his exclusion:

I am glad that Hartington has not joined Mr G. Northbrook writes that he wd. not accept office under him now, even if invited. I should have been glad to take a part in Irish legislation again, if it had been such as I could in conscience approve of, it would have been a great relief to me to earn an official income, but this, as things are, is utterly out of the question, even if Gladstone invites me, which he will not.[4]

One reason that Carlingford took any offer to be out of the question was that he knew Northbrook had shown his anti-Home Rule letter to Spencer and Hartington. Yet on 4 February 1886 Carlingford was considered along with Wolverton and Aberdeen as possible Lords-Lieutenant of Ireland.[5] All candidates were manifestly unsatisfactory, yet it was Wolverton whom the party leaders rejected most peremptorily, and Aberdeen's eventual appointment was not agreed upon till well after all the other important posts had been decided. There is no way of knowing what was said about Carlingford on this occasion, but it is quite

[1] Strachie MSS. H. 338, 3 Jan. 1886.   [2] Ibid. 8 Jan.
[3] Ibid. 8 Jan.   [4] Ibid. 3 Feb.
[5] B.M. Add. MS. 44771, ff. 58, 61.

likely that the general wish to drop him, would have been waived in the circumstances, had he not been abroad and been believed, on the evidence of his own letters and Spencer's and Granville's testimony, to be more resolutely Unionist than the other Unionists who had accepted office. Thus on this occasion Gladstone's desire to be rid of him, might have led him to make an offer of a job for which there were few other takers, rather than the reverse.

Granville wrote on 8 February, and Gladstone on 7 February, putting their obviously embarrassed excuses to Carlingford. Their letters crossed him on his return from Mentone, and he was not able to acknowledge them till 19 February.[1] Gladstone's letter stuck to the single point of the difficulty of negotiating with Carlingford by telegraph: Granville was personally much warmer, argued that 'the H. of Commons men had kicked violently against so many places in the cabinet being allotted to' peers, and added: 'I may tell you secretly to show that Gladstone wd. have been pleased to have you, that he would have telegraphed to you to offer a high office if Spencer and I had been able to give him a confident opinion that you were likely to accept'. Granville was only too aware at this moment of the fragility of the ego among ageing politicians, but the suggestion he offered of a readiness by the Liberal leaders not to recognize themselves as bound by their own view of Carlingford's status, has a ring of truth which need not be reduced to a question of tact.

Carlingford's reply to Gladstone stressed his connexion with 'the great Irish minority' but was otherwise politically conciliatory and avoided giving an impression of categorical opposition. To Granville, however, he revealed the much simpler truth that he was 'obliged to be utterly passive especially avoiding business and head work of all kind'.[2] That this was no routine disavowal, appears from a letter written the next day to his brother saying he was 'totally unfit at present for business or exertion of any kind'.[3]

---

[1] Granville to Carlingford, 8 Feb. 1886, (copy), P.R.O. 30/29/213; Gladstone to Carlingford, 7 Feb. 1886 (copy), B.M. Add. MS. 44123, f. 251; Carlingford to Gladstone, 19 Feb., ibid. ff. 252–3.

[2] Carlingford to Granville, 19 Feb.: Granville MSS. P.R.O. 30/29/28A/1155–6.

[3] Strachie MSS.

This throws as much light as anything else on Carlingford's inactivity as a Liberal Unionist in 1886. It is hard to find any discussion of his position in the archives of other politicians. Yet it is fairly clear that he did not appear at any of the public jamborees or business meetings of the dissident Liberals during 1886. This was partly perhaps personal, in that he had always been much closer to Granville than to Hartington, and he could only have appeared in public on Unionist platforms as an acolyte to Hartington. His name, epitomizing the policy of liberality in Irish government, had much to offer dissident Liberals who were anxious above all to make it clear that it was not the Orange card they were playing. For whatever reason, however, Carlingford remained outside the practical politics of the Hartington secession, though an open letter from him to Hartington on Home Rule appeared in the Irish papers on 8 May 1886, and he was cited by the Liberal Unionist Committee in its pamphlet no. 26 as having declared on 15 May 1886 that 'the proposed measure would be injurious to the Empire and disastrous to Ireland.'[1]

Lord Carlingford died at Marseilles on 5 February 1898, aged 75. It is plain from his journal for 1885 that he was quite capable of finding enough to do looking after his estates, attending to county business, following up his intellectual interests, and cherishing his relatives, especially the growing Strachey family. It is probable that after 1885 this was what he mainly did and what he wanted to do. At any rate his last years were passed outside the public view.

The journal appears to have been written purely for Carlingford's own satisfaction, and without any thought that it might one day be read by someone else. With only himself to please, Carlingford was free to lay aside considerations of relevance and unity, and to write as much of domestic trifles or of his inner broodings, as of the great world of politics. This has affected the way the journal has been edited here.

[1] Carlingford's views were placarded all over Radstock in the 1886 election and a leaflet copy of his letter was sent to every house in this Somerset mining town where he had his colliery. (McMurtie to Carlingford, 3 July 1886: Waldegrave MSS.)

The abridged version of Carlingford's journal published below is roughly half the length of the original. Publication of the whole would probably have been impracticable, and certainly quite pointless, for virtually all the matter omitted can confidently be said to be of no historical interest from any point of view, rather than simply of only slight interest. The vast majority of the excisions made occur in the second half of the year, following his formal resignation of office on 24 June 1885, when he led a life of exceptional passivity. Among matters thus omitted, the topics of the weather, his brother's health, the management of his estates in Somerset and Essex, and the trivial round of daily life among farmers and minor gentry in the country, loom large.

All the footnotes, and all explanatory matter in the text included within square brackets, have been supplied by the editors. Matter within round brackets is as written by Carlingford. A very limited attempt has been made to standardize punctuation.

Contractions and initials occurring in the journal have been printed in expanded form: thus Dss. becomes Duchess, Ly. is given as Lady, wh. appears as which, and sh. as should. Most names of Cabinet ministers appear in the diary as initials. It is left to the context to establish whether D., in any given case, means Dilke or Derby; and whether S. means Spencer or Salisbury. In fact there is perhaps only one passage where any real ambiguity arises. However, since in this version part of the context is sometimes omitted, it was felt that the interests of readers were best served by the expansion of initials as of other abbreviations, where the meaning was not in doubt. The forms 'Mr. G.' for Gladstone and 'Govt.' were however retained as special cases.

The Itinerary of Lord Carlingford in 1885

Jan. 1–27	At Chewton Priory, his Somerset home, with brief visits to Hamilton Place, London.
Jan. 27	To Osborne for a Council: then to Stratton (Lord Northbrook's home in Hampshire).
Jan. 28–Feb. 18	At Chewton Priory, with visits to Hamilton Place.
Feb. 18	To Osborne for a Council.
Feb. 19–Mar. 4	At Hamilton Place.
Mar. 5	To Windsor for a Council.
Mar. 6–26	At Hamilton Place.
Mar. 26	To Windsor for a Council.
Mar. 26–8	At Hamilton Place.
Mar. 28	Left Euston for Ravensdale Park, near Dundalk, the home of his elder brother Lord Clermont.
Mar. 28–Apr. 3	In Ireland with his brother.
Apr. 3–6	In London for a Cabinet.
Apr. 6	Left London for Aix-les-Bains, as Minister in attendance upon the Queen.
Apr. 13	Returned to London.
Apr. 13–May 9	At Hamilton Place.
May 9–18	At Dudbrook, his Essex house, and Hamilton Place.
May 19	To Windsor for a Council.
May 19–26	At Dudbrook.
May 27–June 2	At Balmoral.
June 3	At Warlies, Essex, with Sir Fowell Buxton.
June 4–9	At Dudbrook and Hamilton Place.
June 10	At Weald Hall, Brentwood, Essex, home of C. J. H. Tower, J.P.
June 11–23	At Dudbrook and Hamilton Place.
June 24	To Windsor to resign: then to Hamilton Place.
June 28	Left Hamilton Place for ever: to Dudbrook.
June 28–Aug. 4	At Dudbrook, with visits to London.
Aug. 4	At Bacres, Oxfordshire, home of Henry Grenfell.
Aug. 5	In London.
Aug. 6–Sept. 7	At Chewton Priory.
Sept. 7–9	At Clifton for a meeting.

Sept. 9–15	At Chewton Priory.
Sept. 15–17	At Clevedon for a meeting.
Sept. 17–Oct. 1	At Chewton Priory, with visits to Bristol.
Oct. 1–3	At Somerton Erleigh, home of Col. Pretor-Pinney.
Oct. 3–8	At Chewton Priory.
Oct. 9	Left London for Ireland to visit his brother.
Oct. 9–24	At Ravensdale Park, Dundalk.
Oct. 25–6	In London.
Oct. 26–31	At Chewton Priory.
Nov. 1–3	At Stratton.
Nov. 4–5	At Knoyle, Wilts., home of Alfred Seymour, and Lyme Regis.
Nov. 5–13	At Chewton Priory.
Nov. 13–14	Spoke at Bristol: stayed at Sutton, Somerset, with Edward Strachey.
Nov. 14–19	At Chewton Priory.
Nov. 19	Left Chewton Priory for London.
Nov. 21	Left London for San Remo.
Nov. 22	Entered Italy.
Nov. 30	Taken seriously ill.
Dec. 9	Temperature again normal.
Dec. 31	Still convalescent on the Italian Riviera.
Feb. 12 1886	Returned to London.

Dates of Cabinet meetings, January–June 1885

Jan. 2 Friday
   3 Saturday
   7 Wednesday
  20 Tuesday
  21 Wednesday

Feb. 6 Friday
   7 Saturday
   9 Monday
  11 Wednesday
  16 Monday
  17 Tuesday
  20 Friday
  28 Saturday

Mar. 7 Saturday
  12 Thursday
  13 Friday
  20 Friday
  24 Tuesday
  27 Friday

Apr. 4 Saturday
   9 Thursday
  11 Saturday
  13 Monday
  14 Tuesday
  15 Wednesday
  20 Monday
  21 Tuesday
  25 Saturday
  28 Tuesday

May 2 Saturday
   7 Thursday
   9 Saturday
  15 Friday
  16 Saturday

June 5 Friday
   8 Monday
   9 Tuesday

Informal meetings of ministers also took place on Wednesday, 4 Feb., and on Thursday, 21 May, as well as on several occasions between resignation and the surrender of seals. The status of these meetings defies precise classification.

The Liberal Cabinet in 1885

Prime Minister	W. E. Gladstone
Lord President of the Council	Lord Carlingford[1]
Lord Chancellor	Earl of Selborne
Foreign Secretary	Earl Granville
Home Secretary	Sir W. V. Harcourt
Colonial Secretary	Earl of Derby
Secretary of State for India	Earl of Kimberley
Secretary of State for War	Marquess of Hartington
First Lord of the Admiralty	Earl of Northbrook
Chancellor of the Exchequer	H. C. E. Childers
Lord Lieutenant of Ireland	Earl Spencer
President of the Board of Trade	J. Chamberlain
President of the Local Government Board	Sir C. W. Dilke
Chancellor of the Duchy of Lancaster	G. O. Trevelyan
First Commissioner of Works } Lord Privy Seal	Earl of Rosebery[2]
Postmaster-General	G. J. Shaw-Lefevre[3]

[1] Also Lord Privy Seal until Feb. 1885.

[2] Appointment and admission to the Cabinet announced, 12 Feb. 1885.

[3] Shaw-Lefevre's admission to the Cabinet was announced, 12 Feb. 1885. It involved no change of office.

Extracts, chiefly Political, from the Journal of Lord Carlingford for the year 1885

Thursday 1 January. ... I have begun the New Year in great dejection, possessed with the hopeless want of my own darling woman.

... Northbrook[1] writes in great dissatisfaction about Egypt and Mr G.,[2] and thinks he must resign. I am very anxious about public affairs, and about my own.

Friday 2 January. Went to Northbrook before the Cabinet. He was going to Mr G., invited for the first time since he came back. Walked to ask after O'Hagan[3] (Park Lane) who has had a paralytic stroke.

... Cabinet at 4. Main subject Egypt (as this time last year), and our financial proposals, what to do? France being so slow in replying, and going to make counter-proposals. Gloomy letters from Lyons[4] and Malet,[5] the latter taking a very serious view, going as far as the possibility of a combination of powers, under Bismarck's lead, to turn us out of Egypt or coerce us somehow. The Chancellor[6] even asked whether the fleet was ready. Mr G.

[1] Earl of Northbrook (1826–1904): s. of Sir Francis Thornhill Baring, 1st Baron Northbrook (1796–1866); nephew of Sir George Grey, Whig minister; educ. Ch. Ch.; M.P. Penryn and Falmouth 1857, minor office 1857–8, 1859–66; succ. father, Sept. 1866; Under-Sec. at War Office 1868–72; Viceroy of India 1872–6; cr. Earl, 1876; First Lord of the Admiralty 1880–5; special commissioner to Egypt, autumn 1884, and advocate of single British control there; Liberal Unionist 1886; withdrew from Unionists over tariff reform, 1903; left £203,000 net.

[2] W. E. Gladstone (1809–98); Prime Minister 1868–74, 1880–5, 1886, 1892–4.

[3] Thomas O'Hagan (1812–85), Irish liberal: M.P., Tralee, 1863–5; first Catholic Lord Chancellor of Ireland since James II's reign, 1868–74, 1880–1; in his final years made several private visits to the Vatican on behalf of the British government; d. 1 Feb. 1885 (see below).

[4] Lord Lyons (1817–87), Ambassador in Paris 1867–87: second Baron, cr. Viscount 1881, and Earl 1887; seriously offered the Foreign Secretaryship by Salisbury, July 1886; Catholic convert, 1887.

[5] Sir Edward Malet (1837–1908), Ambassador in Berlin 1884–95.

[6] It is almost certainly Lord Selborne, the Lord Chancellor, who is referred to by this term, and not Childers, Chancellor of the Exchequer. Cf. the statement by Prof. R. F. V. Heuston in his *Lives of the Lord Chancellors 1885–1940* (Oxford,

made a statement and a proposal. He looked unwell and weak, and said with some emotion that he had lost his sleep, and did not know what A. Clark[1] might order—then read his proposal—It was a kind of *sommation* to Mons. Ferry,[2] very stiff, to enter at once upon a discussion of our proposals with Lord Lyons, or else—we should take some new course, and our own course.—But what course? was asked at once especially by Hartington.[3] Mr G. said, he could say if he would, but this not the time for it—the Cabinet had kept together by great forbearance, and he would not bring things to a crisis sooner than could be helped. He showed however that his course would be to 'scuttle' as soon as possible—whether he would make Egypt bankrupt in the meantime, I am not sure. Some of us showed that we could not agree to such a policy—I did so for one. Mr G's memorandum contained concessions which he would authorize Lord Lyons to make—I asked him whether one of these would be our consent to the payment of the interest without reduction.—He was anxious to avoid discussion of that point, but it was clear he would not give way there —would insist on reduction of the interest. There was a long discussion. Nobody liked the proposals, but everybody felt the immense difficulties of the position. (Mr G. said that in the whole of his public life he had never known so difficult a business) and they all acquiesced. Northbrook objected a good deal. I had seen him at the Admiralty an hour before the Cabinet and found him going to Gladstone, the first time that Mr G. had wished to have any talk with him since he came back from Egypt![4] It was agreed

---

1964), p. xv: 'The proper title of the office is therefore that of Chancellor and he is always so referred to in the older and better usage of Whitehall and Westminister.' For Selborne, see below, p. 53, n. 2.   [1] Sir Andrew Clark, his doctor.

[2] Jules Ferry (1832–93): French Premier 1880–1; Premier and Foreign Minister 1883–5.

[3] Marquess of Hartington (1833–1908): succ. father as eighth Duke of Devonshire, 1891, M.P. 1857–91; Sec. for War 1866, 1882–5; P.M.G. 1868–71; Irish Sec. 1871–4; Indian Sec. 1880–2; Lord President 1895–1903; led Liberal Party in House of Commons 1875–80; thrice refused Premiership; leader of the Liberal Unionists in the House of Commons, 1886–91.

[4] Northbrook had returned to London on 2 Nov. 1884. For an account of the Northbrook mission and subsequent Cabinet discussions, see B. Mallet, *Northbrook* (London, 1908), pp. 188–197.

that despatches to Lord Lyons should be drafted, based upon Mr G's memorandum. He then went off to see Andrew Clark . . .

Saturday 3 January. Cabinet at 12. Intended for Derby's[1] colonial questions—but Northbrook began by objecting to some of Mr G's proposed concessions to Mons. Ferry—especially to a *joint guarantee* of a loan which Northbrook contended must lead to a 'dual' or 'multiple' control. Gladstone was impatient but Northbrook stuck to his point 'with great deference' as he said. Then Derby, on New Guinea! evident that Bismarck's sharp practice amounted to breach of faith—a protest to be sent to Berlin. Then St. Lucia Bay, Pondoland, and the Zulu coast. Mr G. made a protest against the doctrine that we are to oppose the settlement of other powers where we are not in possession ourselves, and applied his own doctrine to the Zulu coast, an unfortunate application. Derby did not agree with him, and Kimberley[2] and others, myself included, protested against that coast being left open to the Germans. The question was left open. Mr G. went off to Hawarden, and the Cabinet sat for two hours more upon the drafts of the despatches to Lord Lyons. Mr G's memorandum was greatly softened down. It looked as if he wished to force on a crisis. Then Hartington raised question of sending a force to Suakim to engage Osman Digna,[3] and so help Wolseley.[4] The Cabinet had dwindled, and I went off to Paddington and just caught the 5 train.

Sunday 4 January. . . . It was my darling love's birthday—I was determined to be back for it if possible . . . She would have been

[1] Earl of Derby (1826–93): Colonial Sec. 1858; Indian Sec. 1858–9; Foreign Sec. 1866–8, 1874–8 (resigned in protest against Beaconsfield's Eastern policy); joined Liberals as Colonial Sec. 1882–5; Liberal Unionist, 1886.

[2] Earl of Kimberley (1826–1902): Lord Privy Seal 1868–70; Colonial Sec. 1870–4, 1880–2; Indian Sec. 1882–5, 1886; Lord President 1892–4; Foreign Sec. 1894–5.

[3] Osman Digna (1845–1926), leader of the Mahdist forces in the eastern Sudan captured by British and interned, 1900–24.

[4] Sir Garnet Wolseley (1833–1913): Baron 1882, Viscount 1885; commander of Gordon relief expedition, 1884–5; C.-in-C., Ireland, 1890–5; C.-in-C. of the Army 1895–1900. For his own account of Nile expedition 1884–5 see *In Relief of Gordon* (London, 1967), an edited version of his campaign journal.

64, and how utterly delightful! It is dreadful to think of what an old age she might have had—and that I might have saved her. I was possessed by that thought. Oh! the apathy, and blindness, and self-deception, and self-indulgence, and weak careless confidence in which I had sunk myself at that time! judicial blindness I feel it to have been. Forgive me, my love.

Tuesday 6 January. . . . Found a telegram for a Cabinet—a great bore. And I was anxious, thinking that something decisive might be coming. Went to her grave.

Wednesday 7 January. Up early. Drove in brougham to Bath. . . . London at 12.30. Walked to Downing St. Found Cabinet had been called by Hartington, not by Granville.[1] Question whether a force should be sent to Suakim—a good deal of difference—I was in favour of it. Decided to obtain decided opinion fom Wolseley, and leave discretion with Hartington.[2] Lord Lyons had reported that Mons. Ferry utterly declined to discuss our proposals, but promised his on or before the 15th, and was friendly in tone. Nothing more could be done—and so things are brought back to the point at which they were on Friday, before Mr G's proposal! He made no difficulty about the serious changes made in it before it was sent. There was some talk of what was to be done in the probable case of the French proposals being impossible— Harcourt[3] made quite a new departure for him, and *said he would be prepared to secure payment of the full interest as long as we were*

[1] Earl Granville (1815–91): Colonial Sec. 1868–70; Foreign Sec. 1870–4, 1880–5; Colonial Sec. 1886; leader of the Liberal Party in the House of Lords; Gladstone's closest colleague.

[2] The Cabinet went a little further than this: 'Troops enough will be sent, at all events, to keep Osman Digna employed [i.e. on the Red Sea coast], and prevent him from interfering with Wolseley's operations on the Nile.' It was Baring, not Wolseley, who was pressing hard for a Suakim expedition. (Carlingford to Spencer, 7 Jan. 1885: Spencer MSS.)

[3] Sir W. G. G. V. V. Harcourt (1827–1904): M.P. 1868–1904; Sol.-Gen. 1873–4; Home Sec. 1880–5; Chancellor of the Exchequer 1886, 1892–5; leader of the Liberal Party 1896–8; as a young man he had been close to Lady Waldegrave and might well have become her fourth husband.

compelled to stay in Egypt. Chamberlain[1] protested—said he would allow Egypt to be bankrupt, would announce that we would leave it at the earliest possible moment, but would not permit (?)[2] any other Power to take our place.[3] I entirely differed. Said I was very glad to hear what Harcourt had said—that we were bound to put our hands in our pockets in order to fulfil the task we had chosen to undertake in Egypt and get out of it with credit, that expenditure to enable the Govt of that country to perform its duties and fulfil its obligations, so long as it was in our hands, was quite as justifiable as expenditure for its defence etc. Dilke[4] (just returned from South of France) brought forward case of Samoa, and German conduct there, contrary to engagements with us. Zanzibar also discussed, and agreed that Granville should inform German Govt of our special position and interest there—It was even agreed that it would be impossible to allow any Power to establish itself there, which we do not desire to do ourselves. As to final disposal of Samoa, the idea was that Germany should have it, and we should have Tonga, which is near Fiji! Derby would like to declare British sovereignty over Zulu coast up to Portuguese frontier, but on account of Gladstone's unfortunate dictum[5] nothing was done. Granville was provoking—so difficult to know whether he heard what was said, and intended to act according to decisions come to. He evidently hates tackling Bismarck in any

[1] Joseph Chamberlain (1836–1914): Mayor of Birmingham 1873–6; M.P. 1876; President of Board of Trade 1880–5; President of Local Govt. Board, Feb.-Mar. 1886; Colonial Sec. 1895–1903 (resigned).

[2] The query occurs in the original, presumably indicating Carlingford's scepticism about British omnipotence. All subsequent cases of this usage are as in the original.

[3] Chamberlain had already outlined to Dilke an almost identical Egyptian programme, adding however a final point suggesting an international conference 'to settle at once details of decentralisation as soon as we go' (Chamberlain to Dilke, n.d. [5 Jan. 1885], Chamberlain MSS. JC 5/38/386.)

[4] Sir Charles Wentworth Dilke, 2nd Bt. (1843–1911): M.P. (Lib.) 1868–86, 1892–1911; sought notoriety as republican and radical from 1870; Foreign Under-Sec. 1880–2; President of Local Govt. Board 1882–5 (in the Cabinet); preoccupied with management of Redistribution Bill for most of 1885; from July 1885 his ruin by scandal appeared probable.

[5] For Gladstone's protest against regarding colonization by other powers jealously, see 3 Jan. above.

way. 'If it were not for Egypt, we need not mind him' he said. Kimberley very strong about Bismarck's bullying—would not submit to it etc.—Office.—Dined with Harcourt for the first time for a long while. Lady Harcourt there. . . . Chamberlain said something like an unscrupulous speech he has just made. Derby spluttered out 'In the eyes of some of our colleagues the great crime seems to be to *own* anything.'

Thursday 8 January. . . . Wrote to the Queen . . . The Queen complains to me that some of her Ministers have not written to congratulate on the Princess Beatrice's marriage.

At dinner at W. Harcourt's[1] were Derby, Trevelyan,[2] Chamberlain, Northbrook—some good talk in which Derby took little or no part. Chamberlain repeated his 'bankruptcy' plan—Northbrook very sensible—Harcourt and I agreed against Chamberlain, quite a new thing.

Friday 9 January. This has been a bad day with me, in mind and body. . . . To her grave before luncheon, and some time in the church. I knelt before the memorial of my love, and poured my heart and body out to her—and cried to her for her forgiveness, as I am always doing, for my miserable failure towards the end of our life together, and at the end, to think for her and to help her, to guide and guard her—my love my love—and yet I cannot think it likely that she exists at all—God help me! I have had the wretched feeling of inward sinking badly today—physical sinking and sinking of heart—. . .

Saturday 10 January. . . . Very cheery and confident telegrams from Wolseley.

At Wednesday's Cabinet Hartington said that Chamberlain had asked him (on a former day) a question which he found it

---

[1] i.e. on 7 Jan.: see above.

[2] (Sir) G. O. Trevelyan, (2nd Bt.) (1838–1928): M.P. (Lib.) 1865–86; Irish Sec. 1882–4, breaking down under the strain; Chancellor of the Duchy of Lancaster 1884–5; Scottish Sec., Feb.–Mar. 1886 (resigned); violently anti-Home Rule, Mar.–July 1886; lost seat, July 1886, as Lib. Unionist; returned for Glasgow as a Gladstonian, 1887; Scottish Sec. 1892–5.

very difficult to answer, namely, what he would do in Egypt if the powers reject our proposals—what he meant by talking of a sort of temporary protectorate etc.—just like his courageous truthfulness.

Gladstone's absence made a difference. Trevelyan said a good deal almost for the first time[1]—I found myself saying more than usual.

Sunday 11 January. Stormy day. Twice to church ... I am constantly struck by the strange facts of orthodox religion and services—incredible they will seem some day—for instance that we should be singing the old Jewish song 'Moab is my washpot' etc.[2]

... One of my days of outward peace and inward strife and pain.

Tuesday 13 January. ... To Petty Sessions—Very little business—home before luncheon.

Wednesday 14 January. ... When I read letters of public men, such as Croker's,[3] or a diary such as H. Greville's,[4] I feel what it is that has been all my life my great want both in politics and society—the want of self-confidence. With that I could have done a great deal more than I have done. I should have been much more useful and also happier—Indeed without my darling woman, what should I have done? ...

Thursday 15 January. ... Read a clever and remarkable speech[5] of Chamberlain's (at Ipswich) sketching a Radical policy as to land, education, etc. He (partly followed by Dilke) takes up a position

[1] Trevelyan had entered the Cabinet in Oct. 1884.

[2] Carlingford's position was that of his friend and official subordinate Matthew Arnold: 'The world will have to get on sooner or later without the belief in any supernatural religion, but I do not see how humanity can dispense with religion of some kind.' (Carlingford to Lear, 29 Sept. 1882.)

[3] *The Croker Papers. The Correspondence and Diaries of the late Rt. Hon. J. W. Croker*, ed. Lewis J. Jennings (London, 1884).

[4] *Leaves from the Diary of Henry Greville*, ed. Viscountess Enfield (London, 1883–1905).   [5] See *The Times*, 15 Jan. 1885, p. 7.

quite different from that of the rest of the Cabinet, and from that of a Cabinet Minister with joint policy and responsibility according to the old understanding of that institution. He proclaims his own policy, and bids for the favour of the coming democracy, as if he were an independent politician.

Sunday 18 January.[1] ... Cabinet on Tuesday—for the French answer. Received Waddington's[2] letter to Granville containing it. It proposes an international enquête in Egypt—an international guarantee of a loan—and a conference!

Monday 19 January. ... The other day at Brooks's I overheard Gurdon[3] of the Treasury talking very openly of official matters to West.[4] He spoke with very little respect of Northcote[5] and Childers[6] as Chancellors of the Exchequer,—'weak' etc.—

A letter from Sir Samuel Baker[7] to Mr. Gladstone circulated— earnestly recommending a close 'alliance' with Egypt through the Porte—treating annexation or protectorate as impossible. He says we could not change Tewfik as Khedive for the better.

[1] Carlingford was sixty-two this day.

[2] William Henry Waddington (1826–94): b. in France, s. of an English textile manufacturer who settled there in 1780; educ. Rugby and Trinity College, Cambridge; rowed in university boat race, 1849; followed scholarly pursuits, c. 1850–70; Deputy 1871; Foreign Minister, Dec. 1877–Dec. 1879; Premier Feb.–Dec. 1879, retaining the Foreign Ministry; Ambassador in London, July 1883–March 1893. The *Letters of a Diplomat's Wife, 1883–1900* (London, 1903) by his wife, Mary K. Waddington, is politically uninformative for 1885.

[3] Sir William Brampton Gurdon (1840–1910), Treasury official: entered Treasury 1863; private sec. to Gladstone 1865–6, 1868–74; M.P. (Lib.) N. Norfolk 1899–1910; K.C.M.G. 1882.

[4] (Sir) Algernon West (1832–1921), Chairman of Board of Inland Revenue, 1881–92; cr. K.C.B. by Gladstone, 1886; Gladstone's private sec., 1868–73.

[5] See 20 Feb. below, n. 5.

[6] H. C. E. Childers (1827–96): First Lord of the Admiralty 1868–71; Chancellor of Duchy of Lancaster 1872–3; Sec. for War 1880–2; Chancellor of the Exchequer 1882–5; Home Sec. 1886; early proponent of a version of Home Rule, but conspired against Gladstone's bill, Mar. 1886; a politically isolated figure in the Cabinet; primarily an administrator, but dogged by departmental misfortunes. Cf. the statement in Edward Hamilton's diary, 5 Dec. 1884, that Gladstone confessed to being disappointed in Childers, 'an opinion which is generally shared in the Treasury' (B.M. Add. MS. 48638, f. 83).

[7] Explorer of the Nile, and former officer in the Egyptian service in the Sudan.

Tuesday 20 January. Office. Luncheon at Athenaeum.

Cabinet at 3. Lady Georgiana Fullerton[1] has just died, and Granville evidently felt it very much—could hardly control his voice. First some talk about New Guinea—then the question of the day, the French proposals. The subject was *abordé* in the gradual tentative way so characteristic of the Cabinet. Derby began by asking whether 'international guarantee' of a loan implied international control or interference. Mr G. said certainly not, and quoted some such loans. By degrees the discussion concentrated itself on the international enquête into Egyptian finance. This was strongly opposed by Hartington, Northbrook, and (to my surprise) Childers. Supported *more suo* by Harcourt as perfectly reasonable, a thing the Powers had a right to require, etc.—So also by Gladstone, and admitted by the Chancellor,[2] Kimberley, etc. Childers and Mr G. came into collision in a way very unusual and curious. Childers said 'The truth is, Mr G., that if we had really taken the control of Egyptian finance into our hands, there would have been no necessity for "cutting the coupon" or for a Conference' and he said and showed that he had been in favour of having an English Finance Minister. (This is true, but he did not press it seriously and effectually.) Mr G. grew very impatient, lost his temper, and put the question in a very perverse way. He took the votes, which was quite unnecessary, and took them on the issue—Shall the French proposals be accepted as a basis?—including, as he said when pressed by Northbrook, the enquête.—Upon this, so explained, Hartington, Northbrook, and Childers said No—and I voted with them. The other 8 said yes. Chamberlain was absent, laid up with abscess in the jaw. Then long discussion as to what kind of enquête and how to lessen the objections to it. Northbrook asked questions—for instance—

[1] Granville's younger sister: died 19 Jan. 1885.

[2] Roundell Palmer (1812–95), first Baron (1872) and Earl (1882) of Selborne: M.P. 1847–57, 1861–72; Sol.-Gen. 1861–3, Att.-Gen. 1863–6; Lord Chancellor 1872–4, 1880–5; militant adherent of the Established Church and the landed interest. Selborne's daughter had married the ninth Earl Waldegrave in 1874, and Selborne's relations with Carlingford were coloured by a belief in the injustice and indelicacy of Carlingford's having dispossessed the Waldegrave family of their entire estates during his lifetime.

Must not the reduction of the Land Tax in Upper Egypt, which he had strongly recommended, for the sake of the fellaheen, be postponed and depend on the inquiry?—Mr G. said it might be the first matter to be inquired into! He expected the inquiry to take a year at least! We sat until after 7. . . . Dined with W. Harcourt to meet Gladstone—no other Cabinet man could come. Old Lady Stanley[1] and Lyulph Stanley[2] were there and Lady Harcourt and Lulu Harcourt.[3] Talk at dinner about the crofters. A yellow box came in, and there was significant muttering between Mr G. and W. Harcourt, who went to his room together when the ladies moved. . . . W. Harcourt denounced and ridiculed education, etc.

As soon as Lady Stanley went, W. Harcourt took me into his room looking unutterable things. He supposed I had guessed what that box contained, (which I had),—Hartington's resignation, and Northbrook's through Hartington. He told me all that Gladstone had been saying to him, and a great deal of his own.—Gladstone evidently furious and defiant.—Those who had voted against him must go—He himself would go on—would not resign, even if the Queen desired him to do so—would meet Parliament upon this issue, and stand or fall upon it. (This W. Harcourt's account of Mr G's language.) If he fell, W. Harcourt said (I was going to write 'thought' but 'said' is safer), he could not have a better occasion to fall! He talked of Hartington—sorry to separate from him. This would be fatal to him—would leave the field open for Chamberlain etc. (The other day W. Harcourt was 'determined to break up the Govt'[4] along with Hartington, Northbrook, etc.!) He talked of former difficulties with Hartington—going to resign

---

[1] Widow of Lord Stanley of Alderley (1802–69): P.M.G. 1860–6. Lady Stanley had known Carlingford well since 1847.

[2] Hon. Edward Lyulph Stanley (1839–1925), 3rd s. of the above: Fellow of Balliol 1862–9; M.P. (Lib.) Oldham 1880–5; member, London School Board, 1876–85, 1888–1904; its vice-chairman, 1897–1904; succ. as Lord Stanley of Alderley, 1903, and as Lord Sheffield (in Irish peerage), 1909, using latter title; prominent educationalist and controversialist.

[3] Lewis Harcourt (1863–1922): only s. of Sir W. Harcourt, to whom he was private sec., 1884–5, 1886, 1892; Colonial Sec., 1910–15; cr. Viscount, 1917.

[4] 'Harcourt said on Saturday [i.e. 3 Jan.] that he and some others were "determined to break up the Govt"!' (Carlingford to Spencer, 7 Jan. 1885: Spencer MSS.)

about Candahar (?) and Irish Franchise etc.—I said I was quite ready to share the fate of those with whom I had voted. I did not defend the vote well, not ready enough, as usual. A long time walking up and down his room, while he drank whiskey over the fire—I never feel comfortable with him. How can one trust him? At last I left him and got home at 1.30.

Wednesday 21 January.[1] Had a bad night—full of the uncertainties of the situation—very anxious. Wrote to Northbrook and Childers. A letter came from Granville[2] begging me to do what I could against the resignations ('not that I have any personal interest in it' he added). I answered him that I would.[3] Went to Childers, who was against Hartington's resigning but said he must go with him. Took Childers with me to Devonshire House,

---

[1] The Cabinets of 20 and 21 Jan. were described remarkably accurately in the *Observer*, 25 Jan. 1885, p. 5, writing from the point of view of the dissident minority.

[2] The letters from Carlingford to Childers, and from Granville to Carlingford, have not survived.

[3] Carlingford replied 'I heard last night from Harcourt of Hartington's and Northbrook's intentions, and was distressed to hear it. I entirely agree with you that it is not a difference of opinion which ought to break up the government, and I am going to see what I can do in that sense.

For myself, if the question had been put—Shall we reject the French proposals? I should have voted with Mr Gladstone and yourself. I voted only against the enquête.' (B.M. Add. MS. 44178, ff. 43–4.) Granville, on receiving the above, fairly early in the morning of 21 Jan., sent it on to Gladstone with a covering note (B.M. Add. MS. 44178, ff. 41–2: Ramm, op. cit. ii. 326 (no. 1553)), which he misdated 22 January. The statement that 'Carlingford actually resigned' (Ramm, op. cit. ii. 326, n. 3) bears no relation to the available documents. Carlingford's probably silent dissident vote in Cabinet on Tuesday no more indicated willingness to resign than a dissident vote usually did. He was not a party to, and only learnt by accident about, Hartington's and Northbrook's resignations circulated on Tuesday evening. In the context of a discussion in which Harcourt was trying to impress on Carlingford that Gladstone was itching to force the dissidents out, Carlingford rose to the bait and gave Harcourt the answer the latter sought. But that was late on Tuesday night, and could hardly have been less binding: the following morning Carlingford awoke a man of peace, his anxiety to stop any resignations at all having entirely outmatched his sense of solidarity with the dissidents. The question whether he would have resigned, but for Granville's compromise proposal, at the Cabinet of 21 Jan., cannot be answered with any confidence, but the probabilities on the evidence of that morning alone are rather against than for his doing so.

and found Hartington (who came in with his spectacles pushed up over his head!). I pressed the view that the question of the enquête was not big enough to resign upon, asked him to consider the position of the Moderate Liberals,—asked him if he had a policy for Egypt to announce, etc.—He did not seem absolutely decided, but nearly so. He said that to bring the French to reason, he would run the risk of telling them that we would stay in Egypt as long as we thought necessary, and settle its affairs by ourselves, etc. He said he considered the submission to the enquête *humiliating*. We discussed with Childers what counter-proposal could be made. Then Harcourt was announced, (Hartington saying he didn't want to see him) and Childers and I left, and walked down. I went to Admiralty, stayed with Lady Emma[1] and found Baring[2] waiting for Northbrook who came from Granville's. He said he was determined to resign, could do nothing else, etc.[3] I protested very feebly, really feeling unable to argue against him. Hartington came, and I went to Cabinet at 12.— Granville told me that Mr G. had agreed to a course, which would at all events prevent any resignation for the moment. Long discussion about New Guinea—*Protectorate* or Sovereignty? Derby pressed for the latter, supported by Harcourt, Kimberley, etc. The Chancellor and Mr G. leant to the former, but were convinced by the argument. Then Granville proposed *that we should strongly object to, and argue against, the enquête.*[4] This was accepted by Hartington, Northbrook, Childers, etc. I expressed satisfaction. *W. Harcourt said that no line should be taken which would compel us to break off if the French adhered to their proposal.*

Some talk as to whether the Opposition would take office supposing the Govt. to resign. W. Harcourt and others thought

[1] Northbrook's only daughter. His wife had died in 1867 and he never remarried.

[2] Sir Evelyn Baring (1841–1917), H.M.'s Agent and Consul-General in Egypt 1883–1907: cr. Baron Cromer 1892, becoming Earl 1901; distantly related to Northbrook.

[3] Northbrook had made up his mind to resign whether Hartington did or not. (Carlingford to Spencer, 21 Jan. 1885: Spencer MSS.)

[4] Carlingford's description of this decision is incomplete, because partisan. What happened was that to placate the dissidents, the Cabinet took strong exception to one of the French proposals, while swallowing the others.

not. Derby thought they would. Lord Selborne knew (of course from the Salisbury[1] quarter) that they would consider it a calamity to be obliged to take office. I left Granville settling the mode of putting our objections to Waddington, with Hartington and Northbrook. Childers said it was an extraordinary escape from a breakup, and thought the danger over.

... Dined with Lady Molesworth,[2] there only the H. Reeves[3]

[1] Selborne's son had married Salisbury's daughter in 1883. A large part of the Conservative leadership was in poor health at this time, and Churchill was as far as ever from the ruling circles of the party. Hence even after the débâcle at Khartoum, that most lukewarm of party men, Lord Derby, could write with reasonable complacency 'The opposition probably don't want to come in: they have no leaders in the Commons, and none seem likely to turn up' (to Rosebery, 14 Feb.: Rosebery MSS., box 62). After the Government had narrowly avoided defeat on the Sudan censure motion in Feb. one prominent member of the Tory shadow cabinet commented: 'I think it very fortunate that the Govt. had a majority in the House of Commons. We should have been placed in a very awkward spot if the Govt. had resigned' (Richmond to Cairns 7 Mar. 1885: Cairns MSS., P.R.O. 30/51/3, f. 212.) Akers Douglas, then a junior whip, but shortly to become Tory chief whip, accurately summed up Conservative demoralization before Khartoum fell: 'Systematic and flagrant slackness is the characteristic attitude of the Conservative party but that hardly describes the present policy—not only the goaty brigade but our friends Beach, Raikes etc. seem to be quietly slumbering. Salisbury is indolently enjoying himself in the Riviera and Northcote making rotten speeches. ... I wish our people would pull themselves together and strike out some line of policy which we could place before the country' (Akers Douglas to Churchill, 31 Jan. 1885; Churchill MSS. iv. 552). Salisbury was on the Riviera till 13 Feb.: Churchill was away on a jaunt in India from the beginning of Dec. 1884 to the first week in Apr. 1885.

However, Churchill's closest confidant, Sir M. Beach, warmly applauded the Conservative policy of inaction. While admitting that he had never known 'a more complete lull in politics' on the Conservative side, he went on to point out that 'it would be to our advantage, as a party, to let them go to the country next January as a Government without a popular cry at home, and discredited in every department of administration' (Beach to Churchill 10 Jan. 1885: Churchill MSS. iv. 537).

[2] Andalusia, Lady Molesworth (1809–88), widow of Sir William Molesworth (1810–55), the early Victorian radical leader and M.P.: prominent Liberal party hostess and friendly rival of Lady Waldegrave; her husband left her a life interest in his estates in Devon and Cornwall; a lifelong friend of Carlingford, who noted elsewhere in 1885, 'She is my only link with "the world".' (i.e. polite society.)

[3] Henry Reeve, C.B., (1813–95): clerk of appeals to the Privy Council 1837–53; registrar of the Privy Council 1853–87; leader writer on *The Times* 1840–55, editor of *Edinburgh Review* 1855–95; known to colleagues as Il Pomposo; edited diaries of Charles Greville.

and Gregory.[1] . . . [Gregory] got upon the subject of my darling love by contrast with Lady Molesworth (though very friendly to her) and spoke of her in a way that delighted me—her power over him for good. 'It was she who got me Ceylon, and was everything to me since I knew her. What a different man I should have been, if I had known her earlier!'

Thursday 22 January. . . . Went to see Mundella[2] laid up with bronchitis.[3] Sat with him in his bedroom. Luncheon Brooks's.

Sunday 25 January. . . . Twice to church . . .
. . . The more I think about the proposals of the Powers, the more I hate[4] them—but we have brought them on ourselves, by not having the pluck to settle Egyptian finance ourselves, without the Conference, with all that has come of it. I ought to have opposed the enquête more decidedly than I did. I forgot to say that at the second Cabinet, Trevelyan came round to Hartington and the other three of us, saying he was against the enquête.

Monday 26 January. To London early [from Somerset].
. . . Luncheon at Athenaeum. Then to Childers and Hibbert[5]

---

[1] Sir William Henry Gregory (1817–92): Irish M.P. 1842–7 and 1857–71; Governor of Ceylon, 1871–7; in 1885 owned 5,000 acres in Galway, of annual value £2,400; his interesting autobiography published posthumously, 1894; his second wife celebrated by Yeats.

[2] A. J. Mundella (1825–97): moderate radical M.P. 1868–97, Vice-President of the Council 1880–5; President of Board of Trade and member of Cabinet, 1886, 1892–3; for his career, see W. H. G. Armytage, *A. J. Mundella, 1825–1897: The Liberal Background to the Labour Movement* (London, 1951). For Mundella's view of Gladstone, see entry for 13 June, below.

[3] Mundella was out of action for some time, writing on 10 Feb. 1885 'I have improved so much during the last few days, that I shall be equal to anything I hope a week hence' (Strachie MSS. H. 322). Carlingford had written as early as 16 Jan. inquiring after Mundella's health (Mundella MSS., f. ii). Later in the year Mundella wrote of his poor health as a standing obstacle to his career (Mundella to Chamberlain, 29 Sept. 1885, Chamberlain MSS. JC 5/55/6), and in 1886 he was laid up for most of May and June, again with bronchial trouble.

[4] The previous day Carlingford had written to Edward Lear 'in foreign affairs I sigh for Palmerston.'

[5] John Tomlinson Hibbert (1824–1908), Liberal junior minister: bar, 1849; M.P. (Oldham) 1862–74, 1877–86, 1892–5; sec. to Local Govt. Board 1872–4,

for Education and Science and Art estimates. .... The Treasury
are alarmed at the automatic increase of our votes. Childers told
me that he had been to Paris to see Lord Lyons (the newspapers
did not find it out) and that the negotiation promised well.
... Dined Brooks's. Talked to C. Villiers.[1]

Tuesday 27 January. To Osborne ... The Queen saw me before
Council—full of the dynamite outrage[2]—spoke with displeasure
of Chamberlain's speeches, very naturally—talked of the Royal
Marriage Act, of Lady Waldegrave, Mrs Horton, Mrs Fitzherbert, the Duchess of Inverness, etc.—had no doubt that George
IV had married Mrs Fitzherbert—thought there was something
wrong about the marriage of the Duke of Sussex—had never
treated the Duchess of Inverness as an aunt—*u.s.w.*[3] She asked me
to write her something explaining the Marriage Act.[4]

... A good deal of talk with Northbrook, very happy about
the prospect of the negotiation, and the success of the resistance to
Gladstone—It was Hartington's doing.

Wednesday 28 January. To London early with Northbrook. Read
in the train a MS. book of his containing narrative of all that has
taken place with respect to his Report and Egyptian finance since
he returned.

To Athenaeum. The news came of more successful fighting by

1880–3, Under-Sec. at the Home Office 1883–4; financial sec. to Treasury 1884–5,
1892–5; sec. to the Admiralty, 1886.

[1] C. P. Villiers (1802–98): Liberal M.P. for Wolverhampton 1835–98; Cabinet
minister 1859–66.

[2] Several explosions took place in and around London during Jan. 1885, the
gravest occurring on 24 Jan. at the Tower, in Westminster Hall, and in the House
of Commons. Serious damage was caused and two policemen badly injured, but
there was no loss of life. An indirect victim was Chamberlain, who could not have
chosen a worse moment to launch his first major campaign to radicalize the new
democracy.   [3] *Und so weiter* (German for etc.).

[4] Carlingford had a family connection with this problem, in that in 1766
George III's brother, the Duke of Gloucester (1743–1805), had married Maria,
widow of James, 2nd Earl Waldegrave, formerly governor of George III.
Controversy about this marriage played some part in producing the Royal
Marriages Act, 1773. No correspondence from Carlingford on the subject has
survived in the Royal Archives.

Sir Herbert Stewart's force, and of Stewart[1] being severely wounded—great excitement—. I am not sure that I mentioned the brilliant fight at Abu Klea wells, (on the 17th) against a great superiority of numbers. 'Fred Burnaby'[2] who was one of the killed, is much regretted.

... Northbrook spoke strongly of Mr G's treatment of him since he returned from Egypt, *i.e.* since Mr G. saw his Report. He spoke of Granville as responsible for a great deal of our mistakes—having no policy of his own—making no use as against Gladstone of his position as Foreign Minister, but being entirely used by Gladstone etc. Surprised to find that he had mistaken Childers, who, it seems now, has been against Mr G., but did not assert himself.—

Friday 30 January. A letter from McMurtrie[3] to say that they had reached a vein (a thin one) of good coal in the Middle Pit sinking [at Radstock, Somerset] at a depth considerably less than elsewhere in the district, where pits have been sunk to the second series. This is an important event for the Waldegrave estate, and for Radstock, perhaps for myself. How excited my darling would have been about it!

Monday 2 February. I have disturbed nights and an oppressed head, as I used to have so often here in *our* days—It used to make me gloomy and cold with my darling and I didn't fight against it as I ought to have done.

... Read notice of the *Life and Letters of George Eliot*[4]—that intensely interesting woman.

[1] Commander of column marching on Khartoum: died from wounds, 16 Feb.

[2] Cavalry officer, explorer, balloonist and Conservative candidate at Birmingham in 1880. Had he lived he would have contested Birmingham again in 1885 along with Randolph Churchill and both men would almost certainly have been elected.

[3] James McMurtrie was Carlingford's agent on the Somerset estates of the Waldegrave family, in which Carlingford had been left a life interest by his wife. McMurtrie was especially concerned with developing Carlingford's collieries. He was also a Liberal activist with some advanced views.

[4] *George Eliot's Life as related in her Letters and Journals*, arranged by her husband, J. W. Cross (3 vols., Edinburgh and London, 1885): published the previous week.

... O'Hagan[1] died yesterday—most amiable and likeable man—His second marriage, which my darling much assisted, was a great success for him, though he was old for it.

Thursday 5 February. ... When I got back found a telegram from E. Hamilton[2]—'probably a Cabinet tomorrow. You would do well to come up today'. It was possible to get to London by driving to Bath to a late train, but I did not do it. I did not suspect the cause of the Cabinet, supposing it to be about the French negotiation, or an insolent note of Münster's[3] (Bismarck's) about New Guinea.

Friday 6 February. ... At 7 o'clock Powell brought me the *Pall Mall* saying there was very bad news! It was the news of the fall of Khartoum, Sir Charles Wilson[4] having found it in the hands of the Mahdi, and turned back. Gordon's fate unknown. Never was there a greater disappointment. It is a most lamentable event. Drove to Bath. Read telegrams and articles in the train. Downing St. before 1—but the Cabinet had been sitting since 11—They had decided and sent the telegram of instructions to Wolseley. The question left was what to tell the public and the Khedive. I was very unfit for Cabinet work. ... I am not at all well.

Saturday 7 February. ... Today's Cabinet was unusually unanimous and satisfactory. Hartington read a telegram from Wolseley, by which he very rightly compelled us to decide and say whether irrespective of Gordon *we would destroy the power of the Mahdi at*

[1] See 2 Jan. above. One of his sons, the 3rd Lord O'Hagan, married (1911) a daughter of Lady Waldegrave's niece Constance.

[2] (Sir) Edward Walter Hamilton (1847–1908): Treasury official 1870–1908; private sec. to Lowe, 1872–3, to Gladstone 1873–4, 1880–5; his voluminous diaries, 1880–1906, are in the British Museum; on close terms with his Eton contemporaries Rosebery and Reginald Brett.

[3] Count Münster (1820–1902): German Ambassador in London 1873–Mar. 1885, in Paris 1885–1900.

[4] Maj.-Gen. Sir Charles William Wilson (1836–1905): became commander of the column marching on Khartoum, Jan. 1885, and was blamed for its failure by Wolseley, who disliked him: see p. 148 below.

Khartoum—either at once (which he hardly thought possible) *or in the next cold season*! Harcourt began by saying that he would not do this—upon which the Chancellor with much earnestness said he felt it to be necessary for the credit and influence of England that this *should* be done, and he could not share the responsibility of the contrary policy. That view was strongly supported by Kimberley, then by Derby with unusual fullness and decision—then by all of us. Harcourt's course was curious. He said there was one consideration which led him to modify (reverse) his opinion, viz.—that we had told Gordon to remain at Khartoum, contrary to his own opinion, for the purpose of leaving a settled Govt there. Mr G. raised no objection—though I suspect he had not made up his mind beforehand.—Long discussion of the telegram to be sent to Wolseley followed—and a clear and decided one went. Mr G. said it was 'a momentous decision'.[1]

Sunday 8 February. . . . Sore throat and cough . . .

Monday 9 February. . . . Cabinet at 2. . . . Mr G. announced that Rosebery[2] was about to come into the Cabinet as First Commissioner of Works with the title of Privy Seal, and Lefevre[3] as Postmaster General. (He had written to me about the Privy Seal.)[4]

[1] Carlingford elsewhere described this Cabinet as 'the most satisfactory one there has been for a long time—and even Mr G. makes no difficulty about Khartoum or anything else' (Carlingford to Spencer, 10 Feb.: Spencer MSS.).

[2] Earl of Rosebery (1847–1929): organized the Midlothian campaign, 1879–80; embodied a diffuse Scottish nationalism in early 1880s; Home Under-Sec. 1881–3; Lord Privy Seal and First Commissioner of Works, Feb.–June 1885; Foreign Sec., 1886, 1892–4; Prime Minister 1894–5; resigned party leadership, 1896.

[3] G. J. Shaw-Lefevre (1831–1928), first Baron Eversley of the second creation: M.P. (Lib.) 1865–95; junior office 1868–74; Chief Commissioner of Works 1880–4, 1892–4; P.M.G. 1884–5; President of Local Govt. Board 1894–5; lost seat in 1885 general election and not in 1886 ministry, though a Home Ruler; member of Cabinet, Feb.–June 1885, 1892–5; cr. peer, 1906; in 1885 very much in Chamberlain's pocket, even though Chamberlain regarded him with some contempt (Chamberlain to Dilke, 28 Sept. 1885: Chamberlain MSS. JC 5/24/421).

[4] Rosebery had offered his services to the Government on 8 Feb., in view of the fall of Khartoum, despite his having refused office as recently as 1 Feb. On Granville's suggestion, Gladstone offered Rosebery the office of Lord Privy Seal, then held by Carlingford, as well as Works. The arrangement was approved by Carlingford in a letter to Gladstone on 9 Feb. (B.M. Add. MS. 44123, f. 240), in reply to

Then we had the Suakim expedition—question of Indian troops—
decided to do as Wolseley recommended. Question of the
commander. Wolseley had suggested General Greaves. Hartington said that the Duke of Cambridge was very much against him,
as too junior. Mr G. and Childers strongly against the Duke of
Cambridge.—Hartington said that Wolseley was too much given
to make favourites, and that it had a bad effect to pass over good
senior officers, like Sir Archibald Alison.[1] Wolseley to be consulted. Then Army and Navy Estimates—long discussion. The
proposed increases a good deal cut down, though Mr G. repeated
that 'with his intentions' he felt bound to acquiesce in future
expenditure beyond what he could otherwise have done. Hartington gave up for this year the Military and Commercial Ports, and
confined himself to the fortresses and coaling stations abroad.
Talk about the hostile and insolent language of Bismarck, and
about the French answer on Egyptian finance.

Read at Athenaeum. Dined Brooks's—E. Ashley[2] and H.
James[3] there—the latter asked me to dine at Brooks's to meet
Gladstone.—I was very low.

Tuesday 10 February. Went to Childers at 12. He told me by Mr
G's desire that Mr G. intended to act upon the Report of
Childers' Committee,[4] and separate Education from the Privy
Council. Childers then raised the question whether the office of
Lord President would not then be so nearly a sinecure that it could
not be maintained, but would have to be tacked on to one of

Gladstone's letter dated 8 Feb. assuming—not requesting—his assent to 'the cessa-
tion of the provisional arrangement under which you hold the Privy Seal' (B.M.
Add. MS. 44547, f. 176 (copy)).

[1] Lieut.-Gen. Sir Archibald Alison (1826–1907): s. of the well-known Scottish
Tory historian and man of letters; commander of the British forces in Egypt 1883;
military member of the Viceroy's council, India. 1889–99.

[2] Evelyn Ashley (1836–1907), Liberal politician: M.P. 1874–85, Under-
Secretary at Board of Trade 1880–2, at Colonial Office 1882–5.

[3] Henry James (1828–1911): M.P. 1868–95; Sol.-Gen. 1873; Att.-Gen. 1873–4,
1880–5; refused office from Gladstone, 1886, and became Hartington's closest
adviser; Chancellor of the Duchy of Lancaster 1895–1902; cr. baron, 1895; a confirmed bachelor and confidant of the great; not to be confused with the novelist.

[4] For the report, dated 31 July 1884, see *Parl. Papers*, 1884, XIII, p. 501 et seq.

the other offices. I asked him whether this was Mr G's intention and whether he had told him to tell me so, or to ask me any definite question. Childers said not. I said I had nothing to say, except that I abided by my evidence against the change. Wrote to Spencer[1] ...

Wednesday 11 February. ... Poor Gordon reported to have been killed by treachery. The *Daily News* in mourning.

... There was a Cabinet suddenly summoned.

Thursday 12 February. Gordon's death treated as true by the papers but not officially confirmed. News of severe fighting by General Earle's[2] force—and Earle himself killed.

Announcements of appointments of Rosebery and Lefevre. Rosebery's joining the Govt treated as very important.

Heard from Mundella. He will be disappointed—no room for 'President of Board of Education' now.

I feel my position much changed for the worse. For some time I felt it to be a good one—President of Council and important Irish work in the House of Lords—Now things will be very different.

Childers treated the Presidency of the Council, after losing Education, as a mere sinecure, and I had not presence of mind enough to argue the point with him,[3] as I might have done. Already I feel in Cabinet the great disadvantage of being outside

[1] Carlingford's letter of 10 Feb., in the Spencer MSS., gives an account of the interview with Childers in terms very similar to those above, concluding 'the prospect is very disagreeable.' Evidently the entry of Rosebery and Lefevre into the Cabinet had turned attention again to the question of reducing the numbers in the Cabinet, and eliminating Carlingford by eliminating his office. Carlingford's alarm proved unnecessary as the Cabinet did not take up the subject of the reconstruction of the Lord Presidency.

[2] Gen. William Earle (1833–85): commissioned 1851, commanded garrison at Alexandria 1882–4; led a column of infantry on the Gordon relief expedition, 1884–5; shot while attacking Mahdists at Kirbekan, 10 Feb.

[3] In the event it was only the imminence of a parliamentary question which forced Carlingford to argue the issue (in a letter to Gladstone, 21 Feb.: B.M. Add. MS. 44123, ff. 241–4). His main point was that setting up a separate ministry for education, would reduce its influence in Cabinet 'at a time when the new made minister cannot possibly find a seat in the Cabinet'. Gladstone replied (24 Feb.), proposing to leave the matter unresolved for the time being.

all the great affairs that are discussed. On the whole I am very despondent.

... I find I have spent in 1884 much more than my own income.

Saturday 14 February. ... Telegram to say Cabinet on Monday instead of Tuesday, so prepared for leaving Chewton.

Sunday 15 February. Twice to church. [The sermon touched on Gordon]. ... The sacrifice of self, of the lower self, to man and God is the magic of Gordon as it was of Jesus Christ. I find myself saying 'poor dear Gordon' as in my prayers I say 'the dear blessed Lord Jesus'.

Monday 16 February. Drove once more to Bath, to catch the early express ... Very low and despondent, no hope no spirit, only the desire to do my best and endure.

Luncheon at Brooks's. Cabinet at 2. Question of the Scotch Crofters—stated by Harcourt—and what legislation? The Lord Advocate (Balfour)[1] came—long discussion in which I took part—a good deal of reference to Irish Land Acts. Then Hartington on military measures for Soudan, one is the often talked of and rejected railway from Suakim to Berber.[2] Upon this, Chamberlain raised the question of policy—Does the railway commit us to

[1] J. B. Balfour (1837–1905): M.P. (Lib.) Clackmannan and Kinross 1880–99; Sol.-Gen. for Scotland 1880–1; Lord Advocate 1881–5, 1886, 1892–5; cr. Baron Kinross, 1902; not related to any of the Balfours on the Conservative side; a member of the Episcopal Church in Scotland.

[2] After an inconclusive campaign in the Suakin area, Gen. Graham returned to England in Apr. 1884. In July 1884, materials for 4½ miles of narrow gauge railway arrived at Suakin, and a short line inland, leading nowhere in particular, was duly built. A small British garrison remained at Suakin, with naval support, during the winter of 1884–5, holding the port and a small surrounding area, but without being in a position to contest the Mahdist control of the hinterland. The fall of Berber, the supposed Nile terminus of the line, and lack of finance caused plans for completion of the railway to be suspended, and but for the emotional response to the fall of Khartoum, the subject would have lain in oblivion. However, following the news of that disaster on 5 Feb., the Government announced on 10 Feb. that, pending Wolseley's definitive offensive, probably in the autumn, on the Nile, hostilities would be concentrated in the Suakin area. On 11 Feb. Gen. Graham was appointed to command the expedition, and on the same day was interviewed at the War Office about how to complete the line. On 17 Feb. a

staying at Khartoum?—'not fair' to commit us, etc. Long discussion, but Mr G. adjourned it. Then—what Bills to be
announced?—W. Harcourt mentioned the Scotch Secretary Bill,[1]
and the question of Scotch Education. I said it was a purely 'Home
Rule' question—no educational reasons for the change, etc.
Rosebery advised that it should be put off until the Scotch members
could be consulted.

Read at Athenaeum. Dined Brooks's. Talked to Rosebery
there. He and Lefevre appeared at Cabinet today. Rosebery and
I got on well. Henry Grenfell[2] sat with me while I was dining, and
afterwards.

Tuesday 17 February. Office. Luncheon Athenaeum. Cabinet at
2.30.

Mr G. read from notes an outline of the language which he
thought the Govt should hold on the subject of the Soudan, and

---

contract was placed with Messrs Lucas and Aird for a *standard* gauge line across
the desert. The route had never been surveyed, and was under enemy control:
the costs could not be estimated. Wolseley protested against the much longer
time required to build a standard gauge line (19 Feb.). Despite this, Graham left
London on 20 Feb., arrived at Suakin on 12 Mar., and began building the new
line on 13 Mar., Hartington having written (27 Feb.) pressing for its rapid construction. Within a month of commencing, Graham had built 19 miles of line, as
well as fighting several inconclusive but quite serious battles. On 30 Apr., the
line reached virtually its maximum length, increasing heat thereafter making both
work and patrolling impossible. On 18 May, Wolseley ordered all construction
to cease, Graham having embarked for England on 16 May. On 14 May, at
Wolseley's insistence, Hartington agreed to a policy of tearing up the railway and
retiring to garrison Suakin port, rather than attempting to maintain an 'English
pale' extending for 20 miles into the hills, as the Cabinet had wished to do on 7
May. From 13 Apr., when Hartington warned Wolseley that Russian pressure
might mean cancelling any further advances from Suakin, the fate of the Suakin
railway and campaign was sealed. It is far from clear that it could have succeeded,
whatever the backing, against the climate and the enemy's guerilla tactics.

[1] For a full account of this measure, see H. J. Hanham. 'The Creation of the
Scottish Office, 1881–7', *The Juridical Review* (1965), 205–44.

[2] Henry Riversdale Grenfell (1824–1902), s. of C. P. Grenfell, M.P., by a d. of
the Earl of Sefton: m.d. of H. J. Adeane, M.P. (Lib.); educ. Harrow, Ch.Ch.;
private sec. to Lord Panmure, then to Sir Charles Wood; shared rooms with
Carlingford at 45 St. James' Place, 1853–63; M.P. Stoke, 1862–68; Governor of
Bank of England, 1881; seat: Bacres, Henley, Oxon; wrote account of Lady
Waldegrave for *D.N.B.*; one of Carlingford's four closest friends.

the military operations intended—. It was accepted in the main. Trevelyan and Chamberlain thought it did not make enough of the safety of the troops. It was vague and cautious as to what should be done when we had 'overthrown the power of the Mahdi at Khartoum'—Wolseley's words. Then discussion of Vote of Credit, House of Commons procedure, etc. Then Derby— should the Australian colonies pay the whole expense of New Guinea Govt, and the Imperial Govt nothing? We decided, against the first opinion of Mr G., W. Harcourt, Chamberlain, Trevelyan, that the Home Govt should contribute.

Wednesday 18 February. To Osborne—for a Council—only Kensington[1] and C. Peel[2] with me. H. Ponsonby[3] said he had not seen the Queen for four days—was not sure whether she would see me. 'I was the only one of the Ministers she would see.' She did see me, and talked a good deal. Said she was weak (a feverish cold and high temperature) but had suffered more in mind than in body from these dreadful events. She spoke strongly against the Govt, *mainly against Mr G.* for the delay of the expedition, for not having done their best to save Gordon, etc.—I could not and did not deny that the expedition should have been sent sooner, but I pointed out that Gordon had fallen by treachery, and apparently not in consequence of the delay.[4] She condemned Gladstone's going to the Play just when Gordon's fate was almost certain. (This is a very general feeling. He went with the Dalhousies),[5] and said, 'Does he feel it at all?' She asked if Northbrook

[1] Baron Kensington, in Irish peerage (1835–96): held Household office 1873–4, 1880–5; 1886; M.P. (Lib.) Haverfordwest 1868–85; cr. U.K. peer, Mar. 1886, under same title.

[2] Charles Lennox Peel, C.B. (1823–99): Clerk of the Privy Council 1875–98; in charge of its meetings, and of the Privy Seal.

[3] Sir Henry Ponsonby (1825–95): Maj.-Gen., 1868; private sec. to Queen Victoria 1870–95; see *Henry Ponsonby, Queen Victoria's Private Secretary: his Life from His Letters*, by Arthur Ponsonby, 1st Baron Ponsonby of Shulbrede (London, 1942).

[4] *Queen Victoria's Journal* for 18 Feb. simply noted: 'Expressed my horror, at what had happened. He tried to make some excuse, but it was no use.'

[5] 13th Earl of Dalhousie (1847–87), personal friend of the Gladstone family: unsuccessful Liberal candidate in Liverpool by-election, Feb. 1880, when he declared in favour of an inquiry into Home Rule; lord-in-waiting, 1880–5; Scottish Sec., Mar.-July 1886, outside the Cabinet.

was not sore about the treatment he had received. The Council was very short, only the Proclamation about the Reserves and Militia. The Queen would have nothing else.

Thursday 19 February. . . . Granville made a statement. He was nervous, and read a good deal from notes. He alluded to domestic events which would have kept him away, had it been possible— the death of Campbell of Islay.[1] Salisbury spoke shortly— striking the note of indignation—'Gordon sacrificed to Cabinet squabbles and party tactics'. Shook hands with Ripon on his return,[2] and Sherbrooke[3] on his marriage. Met Dilke, who said he thought we should be beaten in the Commons, that Mr G. wished to be beaten—that he had given up the idea of retiring and reckoned on coming back to office in November!? Rosebery had a prophecy quite the other way from Broadhurst[4] M.P. Walked away with Kimberley.

Friday 20 February. . . . Cabinet at 2. Called to consider the Vote of Censure of which Northcote[5] has given notice. It is in terms which will secure every Conservative vote but which make it impossible for the Radicals and probably for the Parnellites to vote for it, so not intended to turn the Govt out. John Morley[6] will

[1] Granville's second wife was the daughter of Walter Campbell of Islay.

[2] Marquess of Ripon (1827–1909): Lord President 1868–73; Viceroy of India 1880–4; First Lord of the Admiralty 1886; Lord Privy Seal 1905–8; Catholic convert 1874; returned to England, 23 Jan. 1885, and remained rather unwanted by the Liberal leadership till Jan. 1886.

[3] Sherbrooke (formerly Robert Lowe) remarried on 3 February 1885, his first wife having died the previous November.

[4] Henry Broadhurst (1840–1911), trade unionist and Liberal M.P.: s. of a stone-mason, he practised that trade 1853–1872; became trade union leader, 1872; elected M.P. (Lib.), Stoke 1880–5, and elsewhere until 1906; Under-Sec. at the Home Office, 1886; published autobiography, 1901.

[5] Sir Stafford Northcote (1818–87): leader of the Conservative Party in the House of Commons 1876–85; private sec. to Gladstone 1842–5; entered Parliament 1855; held Cabinet office 1866–8; Chancellor of the Exchequer 1874–80; First Lord of the Treasury 1885–6; Foreign Sec. 1886–7; his handling of the vote of censure on the fall of Khartoum disastrous to his standing in the party: created Earl of Iddesleigh, 3 July 1885.

[6] John Morley (1838–1923): editor of *Fortnightly Review*, 1867–82; of *Pall Mall Gazette* 1880–3; M.P. for Newcastle, 1883–95; originally considered 'the member

move words calling for withdrawal from the Soudan as soon as possible. Long discussion as to how best to argue against both motions. Chamberlain very emphatic against any language being used engaging us to set up a Govt. at Khartoum, even bitter against Hartington, who did not wish us to bind ourselves *against* that policy. Trevelyan and Lefevre nervous about their constituents— Trevelyan very pressing that the military policy should be put as much as possible, as necessary for the safety of the troops now in the Soudan—sure that *that* would satisfy great numbers of our friends. Then question of offers of troops by colonies—Derby attacked for a stupid and ungracious telegram sent by the C.O. Hartington called Chamberlain 'sentimental' about the colonies, and these two were pugnacious.

Saturday 21 February. . . . I feel as if I were not living, but—what shall I call it?—waiting for something that does not come. I find my official life very unsatisfactory. I judge myself by a standard and by comparisons which make me greatly dissatisfied with myself. *This* at least would not be the case, if I were in private life. Yet there are strong reasons against giving up office. My love my life, my only hope and strength—I am more desolate than ever—My hopeless loneliness, both outward and still more inward, is scarcely credible.

Sunday 22 February. . . . To Spencer at 5. He had sent Dasent[1] to ask me to come. . . . Spencer wished to tell me what was being done and in contemplation about Ireland. *Mr G. as usual had not said a word to me on the subject.* 1. Visit of the Prince of Wales, which I knew of in Cabinet. 2. Question of Crimes Act—he for partial not entire renewal. 3. Ideas of reform of Irish Govt—

---

for Chamberlain' but broke away on social policy, autumn 1885, then on Irish questions, Dec. 1885; Irish Sec., 1886, 1892–5; Indian Sec. 1906–10; Lord Privy Seal 1910–14 (resigned over entry into war).

[1] John Roche Dasent (1847–1914): private sec. to Carlingford as Lord President and Lord Privy Seal, 1883–5; s. of G. W. Dasent, asst. ed. of *The Times* 1845–70; nephew of Delane, for whom he worked briefly, 1870; entered education dept., 1876; private sec. to Spencer 1880–2, 1885, and to Kimberley 1892–5; asst. sec. to the Board of Education 1900–8; kt. 1908.

Lord Lieutenancy to be abolished—Secretary of State for Ireland to be substituted, who *should be a peer*, and should reside, as a rule, in Dublin (at all events at first) even during the session. I objected that Ireland would then be represented only by an Under-Secretary in House of Commons, and said I thought that the Secretary of State should be in the House of Commons. To this he made little or no answer. Does this idea concern *me*?

He spoke strongly of the injury and insult to which the Crown was exposed through the Viceroy, who should no longer be interposed between Ireland and the Sovereign. There should be a regular royal residence.[1] He had spoken to W. Harcourt and to Chamberlain about the Crimes Act—the former violent for renewing every jot and tittle of it, the latter of course the other way but moderate. Spencer wishes for more powers against the newspapers, but does not expect to get them. He was going off to Dublin, anxious about his brother.

Spencer talked of the probable successor of Cardinal McCabe[2] being Dr Walsh,[3] President of Maynooth, clever man, extreme

[1] Spencer was very much in earnest about establishing an Irish equivalent of Balmoral, preferably well away from Dublin, and about separating the Lord-Lieutenancy from English party politics, the relation between the two proposals being obscure. Spencer made a passing reference to both projects when outlining his programme of remedial legislation for Ireland to the Cabinet on 28 Apr. 1885, but there is no record of the topic having been argued in Cabinet, presumably because it was a matter for the Queen to decide. In an interview at Windsor in early May, the Viceroy was at first able to win royal approval for turning the viceregal lodge into a palace, and for making the Lord-Lieutenancy a chiefly social office. By 11 May, however, the Queen had come out flatly against all essential aspects of Spencer's plan, which therefore never reached the Cabinet: 'I feel inclined to throw up my sponge and retire to my plough in Northamptonshire' Spencer wrote to Ponsonby (11 May). See Sir Sidney Lee, *King Edward VII, A Biography* (London, 1925), i. 223. However, such subsequent lords-lieutenant as Aberdeen (1886), Londonderry (1886–9), and Houghton (1892–5) were almost purely social figures.

[2] Edward McCabe (1816–85): educ. Maynooth 1833–9; usual ladder of promotion, 1839–77; auxiliary Bp. of Dublin 1877–9; Archbp. of Dublin 1879–85; Cardinal, 1882; condemned Land League and refused to take militant part in pressing claims of separate system of Catholic education, thereby incurring much open criticism from Nationalist clergy (including his successor, Walsh).

[3] William John Walsh (1841–1921): Professor of moral and dogmatic theology at Maynooth 1867; vice-president of Maynooth 1878, president 1880; elected Vicar Capitular of Dublin (i.e. acting head of the diocese), 13 Feb. 1885; nominated

Nationalist politician, chosen 'Vicar Capitular' (?) by the Dublin Chapter, as against the moderate Bishop Donnelly,[1] the Cardinal's right hand man. The latter had called on Spencer, greatly pleased by a telegram from the Queen, and a letter from Spencer on the Cardinal's death. He laid these before the Chapter, and proposed that something proper should be written—but they at once refused—a bad sign—Kenmare[2] knows moderate priests who are strongly opposed to Dr Walsh and hope that the Pope may be induced to choose Bishop Donnelly.

To Athenaeum. Wrote[3] to Mr G. about the Education Department and Report of Committee . . . H. James and I were the only diners [at Brooks's] when Hartington came, of whom we had just been talking.

Tuesday 24 February. . . . The debate on Northcote's motion of censure began yesterday—a great deal of speculation and doubt as to the result. Sir Stafford Northcote said to have made a very bad speech.

This day the Closure was used for the first time against the Parnellites, who opposed the usual motion postponing other business to make way for the Vote of Censure debate. O'Brien[4]

Archbp. by the Chapter, 10 Mar. 1885, defeating Bp. Donnelly by 42 votes to 12: his appointment opposed at Rome by the unofficial British representative, George Errington (see below, 24 July, n. 1), but finally authorized, 23 June 1885, following a visit of seven Irish bishops to Rome; assiduously courted by Conservatives, 1885–6, with offers of a new deal for Catholic education; supported Gladstone's Home Rule Bill, 1886, being consulted by Childers over details of the legislation; see Patrick J. Walsh, *Life of William J. Walsh* (Dublin, 1928). Granville stated that 'Spencer and many of the leading Irish Liberals, Catholic as well as Protestant, believe Dr Walsh to be an able but very dangerous man' (Granville to Chamberlain, 2 May 1885; Chamberlain MSS. JC 5/36/15).

[1] James Donnelly (1823–93): Bp. of Clogher since Jan. 1865; auxiliary Bp. of Dublin under McCabe; liked to describe himself as 'the last of the Whigs'.

[2] Fourth Earl of Kenmare (1825–1905), Irish Whig with large estates in Kerry: held Household office, 1872–4, 1880–5, Feb.–Aug. 1886, continuing in office despite his wish to resign over Home Rule.

[3] B.M. Add. MS. 44123, ff. 241–4, dated 21 Feb.

[4] William O'Brien (1852–1928), Irish nationalist leader: editor of *United Ireland*, 1881; M.P. Mallow 1883–5; imprisoned 1881–2 and 1887; escaped from arrest to U.S.A., 1890; parliamentary career continued till 1918. The motion for his suspension was carried by 244 to 20 (*Hansard*, vol. 294 cols. 1186–8).

called out 'We'll remember this in Ireland', and was suspended. Many of the Conservatives in their blind and stupid hostility to the Govt refused to support the Speaker, and the necessary 200 was only obtained with 7 votes to spare.[1]

Hartington said at Brooks's that he did not see what he could find to say in defence of the Govt. Henry James had been talking of the speculations about a Coalition Govt. of moderate Conservatives and moderate Liberals, including Hartington—which are absurd.

Wednesday 25 February. Office after luncheon. Deputation from School Board of London. . . . It was to ask for more help for evening schools. Mundella did most of the talking. I felt the disadvantage of not being in daily contact with these questions. Talk with Trevelyan. He doubts our having a majority.

Thursday 26 February. . . . Salisbury[2] moved Vote of Censure in an able sarcastic speech—then Lord Wentworth,[3] then Northbrook. He had been saying to me beforehand 'I can't answer this', etc. He spoke with difficulty, with no flow or dexterity, but with sense and courage, and made some good points. He was very nervous, and when he sat down could hardly speak, exhausted by the effort.

Friday 27 February. When I went back to the House of Lords on Thursday night and Harrowby[4] was speaking, Granville asked me, through Kimberley on the bench, if I would speak for ten minutes, the object being that the other side should begin next day—I declined, not having anything ready or anything in Harrowby's speech worth answering.

[1] The actual figures were 207 to 46.

[2] Marquess of Salisbury (1830–1903): Prime Minister 1885–6, 1886–92, 1895–1902.

[3] Lord Wentworth (1839–1906), later 2nd Earl of Lovelace: not a member of the Conservative leadership.

[4] Earl of Harrowby (1831–1900): M.P. (Palmerstonian) 1856–60, (Cons.) 1868–82; succ. father, 1882; as Viscount Sandon, Vice-President of the Council 1874–8 (outside the Cabinet); President of Board of Trade 1878–80, in the Cabinet; Lord Privy Seal and member of Cabinet, 1885–6; in later life an invalid.

... Granville made a good spirited speech, and Salisbury answered well. Division 180 odd to 60 odd.[1] I went then to House of Commons. Heard Forster,[2] as he sat down, announcing that he would vote against the Govt 'because he saw no hope of the Govt doing any better in the future than they had in the past'. Then heard Hartington—a most difficult speech, which did him great credit, a manly speech, like a leader and making the best of his case. Watched the division. The Parnellites came in late, sat in a body, waited until the last moment, then rose together, and walked out into the opposition lobby—not a pleasant sight. Great anxiety about the division—majority of 14 for Govt.[3] Walked home.

Saturday 28 February. Sent for *The Times* before I got up. Upon a second division (Lord G. Hamilton's[4] motion) Govt had majority of 22.[5] Luncheon at Athenaeum. Cabinet at 2. Overtook Kimberley, who thought Mr G. meant to resign. He came in late, and began, 'Well are you talking over the course we are to take etc?'

Harcourt then declared solemnly and at length for resignation—so did Chamberlain—Govt and Party now united, not likely to continue so etc—so Granville, Derby, and Hartington—Then Mr G. stated great doubts whether we should be justified, having got majority of 22 etc. I said our danger lay in yielding to the

---

[1] In fact 189 to 68. Granville in his speech emphasized that the Government was now committed to the 'long or permanent retention of the Soudan' (*Hansard*, vol. 294 cols. 1578–88).

[2] William Edward Forster (1818–86), a former Quaker and Bradford woollen manufacturer: M.P. (Lib.) Bradford 1865–86; junior office 1865–6, 1868–70; in Cabinet, as Vice-President of Council, 1870–4; Irish Chief Secretary 1880, resigned May 1882 over the Kilmainham treaty and was thereafter Gladstone's bitterest opponent inside his own party. For his speech of 27 Feb. see *Hansard*, vol. 294, col. 1699, the concluding passages being accurately summarized by Carlingford.

[3] Northcote's motion was defeated by 302–288.

[4] Lord George Francis Hamilton (1845–1927), 3rd s. of 1st Duke of Abercorn: M.P. (Cons.) 1868–1906; Under-Sec. for India 1874–8; Vice-President of Council 1878–80; First Lord of the Admiralty 1885–6, 1886–92; Indian Sec. 1895–1903 (resigned); left £53,000.

[5] In fact this was the third division taken on the night of 27–8 Feb. in connection with the Sudan. The voting was 277 for the motion to 299 against. In the second division the Govt. had a majority of 343 (*Hansard*, vol. 294, col. 1726).

temptation to run away, and I did not think we should be justified. Spencer and Childers for resignation. Kimberley and Dilke strongly against it, also Trevelyan. The discussion went on for a long time. We seemed more than once *out*, then *in* again—Mr G. declared himself ready to abide by the decision of the Cabinet, but was plainly anxious not to resign. W. Harcourt wavered in the strangest way, but gave up his opinion. So did Chamberlain. At last Mr G. put it to the vote. 'Under all the circumstances, are you for going on?'

Yes—Kimberley, Lefevre, Trevelyan, Harcourt, Dilke, Chamberlain, and myself. *No*—Granville, Derby, Hartington, Lord Selborne, Spencer, Northbrook, Childers. *Rosebery would not vote*! Mr G. gave the casting vote for staying in office. It was no casting vote in fact because he had already brought round W. Harcourt and Chamberlain, and 'Under all the circumstances' meant 'considering how anxious the Prime Minister is to stay in'.

Granville was disappointed and annoyed—said he had understood from Mr G. that he would resign. He had no doubt brought Spencer over, who went back to Dublin disappointed. The Ministers who wished to escape were those who have the greatest difficulties.—We sat until near 7. All the Cabinet dined with me— Sheriff's dinner—except Chamberlain and Lefevre. Sydney[1] and Kenmare dined also, and Peel and Suff.[2] [*sic*]. I had Mr G. and the Chancellor on each side of me. Granville very sulky. Mr G. talked a good deal.

At my dinner, Mr G. talked of George Eliot and Lewes— thought her character became lower than it had been before (?)— seemed incapable of doing her justice. He mentioned Bishop Stubbs,[3] and I told him the story of his marriage. That night I

---

[1] Lord Sydney (1805–90): held Household office 1841–6, 1852–8, 1859–66, 1868–74; cr. Earl, 1874; Lord Steward 1880–5, 1886.

[2] Probably Baron Suffield (1830–1914): held Household office 1868–72, Feb.– Aug. 1886, 1901–10; offered resignation over Home Rule, Apr. 1886.

[3] William Stubbs (1825–1901), historian: vicar of Navestock, on the Waldegrave estates in Essex, 1850–66, where he married the village schoolmistress in 1859. She had been a pupil of his, and was the daughter of Lady Waldegrave's gamekeeper and sister of her gardener (Hewett, . . . *and Mr. Fortescue*, 154). Stubbs was also tutor to Algernon Swinburne: Regius Professor of History at Oxford, 1866–84: Bp. of Chester, 1884, and of Oxford, 1888.

asked Northbrook if he had heard of Mr G's treatment of me in the matter of Constantinople and Rosebery—He said he had and added 'But you are a man who forgives easily' (or something like that).

Wednesday 4 March. Office. Walked. Read at Athenaeum. Looked at a book on Messianic prophecies etc by Edersheim,[1] and then at James Martineau's[2] new book on Ethics—felt the infinite distance between the two subjects, and the solemn realities of the latter. As usual, I am perplexed about the sexual laws—In practice I am as faithful to my darling woman since I lost her, as I was for so many years before I won her.

Dined with the Kimberleys. . . . Lady Kimberley talked in her queer way—abused Kimberley for his Radicalism—said with apparent seriousness that their marriage had been a mistake, but it couldn't be helped now! abused Gladstone of course. Lady Enfield[3] and I somehow got on the Book of Daniel, and she was sternly orthodox on its early date and clear predictions.

Thursday 5 March. To Windsor for a Council—Sydney, Rosebery, Trevelyan, Kensington, and Peel the party in our carriage. In train to Windsor, à propos of the Durham divorce case,[4] Lord Sydney talked of sexual insanity, Lady Lincoln's case,[5] etc., and of families remarkable for sexual passion—one the Harrowby family—one lady of it went out of her mind and was cured by marriage. Old Harrowby, lately dead, 'had women to the last'.

[1] Alfred Edersheim, *Prophecy and History in relation to the Messiah. The Warburton Lectures for 1880–84*, (London, 1885).

[2] Probably James Martineau, *Types of Ethical Theory* (2 vols., Oxford, 1885).

[3] Alice, d. of 1st Earl of Ellesmere: in 1854 she m. Viscount Enfield (1830–98), later 3rd E. of Strafford; her husband a Lib. M.P. 1852–74, and held junior office 1865–6, 1871–4, 1880–2.

[4] Lord Durham's action against his wife on the grounds that she was insane when he married her in 1882, was dismissed with costs on 10 Mar. 1885 (*The Times*, 11 Mar. 1885).

[5] In 1848 Lady Lincoln ran off to Italy with Lord Walpole. Gladstone, as Lincoln's friend, quixotically set off in pursuit, disguised, and located her, pregnant. A bill of divorce was passed in 1850. The injured husband, then Duke of Newcastle, was Carlingford's superior at the Colonial Office, 1857–8, 1859–64, and an admirer of Lady Waldegrave.

I had the Privy Seal in my hand in its case and Rosebery said it looked like an accordion. ... With the Queen for some time. Talked of the Ministerial crisis—she gave me the impression of being disappointed at Mr G. not having resigned. A good deal about Russia. She had written herself to the Emperor. 'Russia is our real enemy' she said, 'I told your Govt what would happen if you gave up Candahar' and so on. I would not admit that to have been a mistake.[1] Kimberley says the mistake made was in stopping the railway—it would and ought to have been at least to Quetta by this time.[2]

Rosebery went through the farce of being sworn in as Lord Privy Seal.

Saturday 7 March. Office. Trevelyan much troubled about Wolseley's telegrams and the Berber railway. We lunched together at Athenaeum. Emly[3] joined us. Trevelyan had been reading the F.O. précis of the Egyptian business. His reflection was 'How bad Gladstone is as a foreign minister! and what splendid success in home politics!' He spoke of his attachment to Hartington, but thought he ought to have resigned or forced the expedition to rescue Gordon sooner.—Cabinet at 2. A long one. Wolseley's telegram insisting on some 45 miles of the Nile railway above Wady Halfa as essential to an autumn campaign was the great subject, and had produced a great effect. W. Harcourt laid it down that there would never be an expedition either to Berber or Khartoum—that within 3 months Wolseley would himself advise the abandonment of the whole thing, etc. Chamberlain

[1] The Queen wrote 'I held a Council after luncheon. Saw Lord Carlingford and talked to him about Russian affairs: upon this subject he says Mr Gladstone is very firm.' (*Queen Victoria's Journal*, 5. Mar.)

[2] Cf. Kimberley to Dufferin, 6 Mar. 1885: 'I am sorry to see that the official report of the Quetta Railway shows that the engineering difficulties are great, and that it will be at least two years before the line will be ready for use' (Dufferin MSS., Public Record Office of Northern Ireland, D 1071 H/M1/3, p. 31). In April, however, Dufferin expected the railway to be ready by August (Dufferin to Kimberley, 18 Apr.: ibid., p. 15).

[3] William Monsell, Lord Emly (1812–94): Catholic convert (1850) and Irish whig; M.P. Limerick 1847–74; held junior office 1857, 1866, 1868–71; P.M.G. 1871–3; cr. Baron, 12 Jan. 1874; Vice-Chancellor of Royal University of Ireland, 1885–94.

was very trenchant, and said he could no longer support the Suakim-Berber railway—Dilke the same. He said this was a time when a man ought to have the pluck to speak out—that public opinion would not allow this long delayed and hazardous campaign to go on, for a purpose in which the country would feel no interest—that for himself he was ready to take the responsibility of abandoning it at once—today. Long discussion. Decided to question Wolseley further—telegram agreed upon.

Then long statement from Granville—his conversations with Herbert Bismarck—Cameroons—New Guinea—St. Lucia Bay etc.—then the financial arrangement of Egypt, *depending on Bismarck*, then what to be said to Fehmi Pasha?[1]—Granville rightly anxious to secure the friendship of the Sultan, and prevent him from thowing himself into the open arms of Russia—but what to do?—admit Turkish troops at Suakim for one thing? W. Harcourt violent against this. Admission of the Turk to Egypt *or the Soudan* intolerable and 'vital' to him—I have never heard him more unreasonable, and he harangued and repeated himself at wearisome length. Some compromise at last arranged. Then the Niger and the National African Company's Charter. W. Harcourt began to declare against the thing, but Chamberlain stopped him—said the commerce of the country would never forgive us if we failed to secure the Niger. Read at Athenaeum Lucy's *Diary of the Parliament of 1874-80*[2]—I was living then—Dined at home.

Monday 9 March. . . . Things look very dangerous on the Afghan frontier—Russian very threatening and aggressive—Sir Peter Lumsden[3] telegraphs that the Russian are trying to provoke the Afghans to fire the first shot, and that the passive attitude which we have forced upon the latter cannot be maintained.

[1] One of the two Turkish envoys in London.

[2] H. W. Lucy, *A Diary of Two Parliaments:* Volume One, *The Disraeli Parliament, 1874-80* (London, 1885).

[3] General Sir Peter Stark Lumsden (1829-1918): entered Indian Army, 1847, rising to Chief of Staff, India, 1879; British Commissioner for demarcation of north-western boundary of Afghanistan, 1884-5; generally distrusted by Liberals as a Russophobe.

Tuesday 10 March. Today at breakfast my name caught my eye in the *Daily News*, and I found it was an article, not editorial, headed 'The Ministry, by a Radical' calling for a weeding of the Cabinet and promotion of Chamberlain, Dilke, and Trevelyan to high offices—Harcourt to be Chancellor. It was insulting to several others, but specially so to me, and attacked me at the greatest length—'no force of thought or character'—once the husband of a 'great lady' whose salon had political influence, reached the Cabinet by her means, and because I was supposed to have a knowledge of Ireland—but should not be got rid of. Why should Mr. Dodson[1] be thrown overboard and Lord Carlingford kept? etc. Nothing could be more contemptuous, insolent, and brutal. Is it Labouchere?[2] very likely—but it is Hill's[3] act. How impossible that he should have done it in my darling's time! This troubles me more than it ought to do. I had lost hold before of the amount of self-confidence that I had gained since I took office, and I am in bad condition for an attack of this kind. I know that there is truth in my want of 'force of thought or character' but I have *enough* to have been able to do my work well in office, and House of Lords. I have no doubt that my Irish work there during '81, '82, and '83 is forgotten, and Mr G's treatment of me in the autumn has had a very injurious effect.

. . . Woke in the night and read the story of Mrs Carlyle's death, which affects me greatly. I think of my lost love, of my miserable dreadful insensibility and blindness. I suffer for it, as I deserve, deeply, bitterly, daily, nightly, though I have seldom mentioned it in this diary. I am more desolate than ever.

Wednesday 11 March. . . . Office. Mundella came—we had a long

---

[1] J. G. Dodson (1825–97): M.P. (Lib.) 1857–84; deputy Speaker 1865–72; financial sec. to the Treasury 1873–4; in Cabinet 1880–4 as President of Local Govt. Board (1880–2) and Chancellor of the Duchy of Lancaster (1882–4); retired from Cabinet, Oct. 1884, becoming 1st Baron Monk Bretton, to make way for Trevelyan. His willingness to retire made Carlingford's refusal to do so stand out in sharp relief.

[2] Henry Labouchere (1831–1912), journalist and political intermediary: M.P. (Lib.) 1867–8, 1880–1906; proprietor and editor of *Truth*, 1876–1905; disreputable, abused, incorruptible, and an invaluable source of information, some of it true.

[3] Frank H. Hill, editor of the *Daily News* 1870–861.

talk about office matters as well as politics and the prospects of the Govt. He said he thought he should resign, if Scotch Education were transferred to the Scotch Secretary. Rosebery intriguing for it among Scotch members. (Rosebery and I are now on easy, talkative terms, which we were not.)

Thursday 12 March. A cup of coffee at Brooks's, on my way to the Cabinet, at 12. A talk about Dover House, just fallen to the Woods and Forests.[1] Should it be used as an official house for the Prime Minister? Mr G. decidedly against this (though he said it could not concern him personally) because it would oblige the Prime Minister to receive—so also Kimberley and Chamberlain— Granville, Rosebery, Lefevre etc. in favour of it. W. Harcourt said the Prime Minister ought to have title and salary[2] of Privy Seal in addition to his £5,000. Childers said he had strong opinion that the P.M. should be also President of the Council 'as it was now decided to take away Education from the President of the Council' (never yet mentioned in the Cabinet), there would be nothing for him to do, and he appealed to me. I did not agree, but of course did not argue it on this occasion. Childers provoked me with his self-satisfied meddling ways. The question adjourned—a curious conversation. Then Wolseley's Proclamation, and title of Governor-General of the Soudan—the former very oriental— both greatly disliked by Mr G., Dilke, Chamberlain, etc. Harting-ton said Wolseley had recourse to such a Proclamation, because he was not allowed to tell the people of the Soudan anything about our intentions, and he thought it a fair translation into English-Arabic of the language held by the Govt in the House of Commons! This was very good.[3]

This was solemnly repudiated by Mr G. Decided to tell

[1] Dover House was later used to accommodate the new Scottish Office, set up in Aug. 1885.

[2] Since 1883 the office of Lord Privy Seal had in fact been unsalaried.

[3] Carlingford had given his opinion in writing the previous day when a memorandum on the subject was circulated by Granville. He wrote: 'to overrule Lord Wolseley as to measures which he considers of great importance for the safety of his army and the success of his operations is a heavy responsibility. I do not see that his temporary assumption of the title would commit the Govt. to anything'. (Granville MSS. P.R.O. 30/29/145.)

Wolseley that in our present critical relations with Russia, Govt did not wish to commit itself further in the Soudan. Hartington raised question—how to justify the attack on Osman Digna, if there was any likelihood of our *not going on*? very hard to answer. W. Harcourt asserted that there never would be a Soudan campaign. Then long discussion of the situation with Russia. W. Harcourt very vociferous and unreasonable. Hartington said to him 'Now I bet a 100 to 1 you haven't read any of the papers' which he could not deny. Answer to Russia prepared by Kimberley and a committee considered.

Friday 13 March. . . . Cabinet at House of Commons to consider a draft despatch and memorandum *in answer to Russia*—very critical matter. Bismarck has refused to sign the Egyptian Convention at the last moment, raising difficulty about the stoppage of the Sinking Funds by Northbrook.

Monday 16 March. [At dinner.] . . . Mrs. Gladstone described the arrival of the news of the fall of Khartoum at Holker where they were staying, and their going off to London by first train in half an hour.[1]

Thursday 19 March. . . . Worked at Poisons Bill. Made statement on its 2nd Reading.[2] No debate and hardly any attention. They did not know what an embarrassing subject it is . . .

Friday 20 March. . . . Cabinet at 2. Derby stated case of Bechuanaland, and quarrel between Sir Hercules Robinson[3] and Sir Chas.

---

[1] The telegram announcing the fall of Khartoum reached Hartington and Mr and Mrs Gladstone on 5 Feb. 1885 at Holker Hall, Lancashire, where they were guests of the Duke of Devonshire. Gordon's fate was still uncertain at the time.

[2] *Hansard*, vol. 295, cols. 1662–5. Under Carlingford's bill all poisons had to be clearly labelled, and enforcement was to be the responsibility of the Privy Council, whereas under previous legislation it had lain ineffectively with the Pharmaceutical Society. In the debate one peer complained that the bill had only been printed the day before.

[3] Colonial governor 1859–80: Governor of Cape Colony and High Commissioner for S. Africa, 1880–9, 1895–7; cr. Baron Rosmead, 1896.

Warren.[1] A telegram agreed upon. Then long talk about Russia and the Afghan question, though nothing to be done or decided at present—except indeed the despatch of 25,000 men (proposed by Dufferin[2] and his Council) through the Bolan to Quetta,[3] before the hot season begins.

I did not expect Chamberlain to do so, but he said he was all for showing a bold front, whatever course we might take in the end. Childers stated the deficiencies of the year '84–'5, and the estimated deficiency of 1885–6, also the amount of the Vote of Credit which must be obtained for the Soudan expeditions—I think £7,000,000. Gladstone groaned. Then talk about the Turks. How to give some gratification to the Sultan, without doing harm etc.

Monday 23 March. ... Received deputation from the Town Council and members for Edinburgh against the Heriot's Hospital[4] scheme of the Scotch Endowed Schools Commissioners. Mundella tried my patience, with his loud pushing ways and bad taste—his great anxiety on such occasions is to make himself the important personage.

Tuesday 24 March. ... Cabinet at House of Commons.

Difficulty about the Egyptian Financial Convention, to come before the House of Commons on Thursday! The two Turkish Ambassadors here could get no power from the Porte to sign. Decided to take a very strong line with them and at Constantinople, to say that they would be given their passports at once if they did not sign according to promise, and that our policy would

---

[1] Sir Charles Warren (1840–1922): general, Palestinian archaeologist, and Chief Commissioner of Metropolitan Police (in 1886–8); sent out from England to settle difficulties arising from Boer settlement in Bechuanaland, 1884, which he did with credit and without bloodshed; recalled, Sept. 1885, leaving an organized police force behind.

[2] First Marquess of Dufferin and Ava (1826–1902): Chancellor of the Duchy of Lancaster 1868–72; Gov.-Gen. of Canada 1872–8; Ambassador in St Petersburg 1879–81, in Constantinople 1881–4; Viceroy of India 1884–8; Ambassador in Rome 1888–91, in Paris 1891–6; a friend of Carlingford since 1849, and once a member of Lady Waldegrave's circle of rising young politicians.

[3] For tel. to Dufferin, sent 4.30 p.m., announcing this decision, see Dufferin MSS. D 1071/H/M1/7, p. 4.   [4] An Edinburgh school: see 27 Mar. below.

be directed to the separation of Egypt from Turkey, if the Sultan treated Egypt in this way. Granville sent for Musurus.[1]

A good deal of talk about the Russian question—the powerlessness of our navy against Russia—Cronstadt impregnable—the Black Sea closed to us unless the Porte should become our ally— Russian exports and imports would pass through German ports. The Chancellor was full of this view.

Thursday 26 March. . . . To Windsor at 1. Hartington, Sydney, and Peel with me. . . . The Queen saw me before the Council—said that Mr G. was sound about the Russian question and 'better' about the Soudan—spoke of W. Harcourt as the one who wanted to run away—told me, laughing, of a scene between him and Lady Ponsonby at his own house, in which he grew so violent that she (I think) left the house.

. . . Granville came down and had long audience. Gave him a lift from the station. He said we were playing for a very high stake with Russia, and if we lost he doubted that we could pay— so hard to make any great impression on Russia by the navy, etc. Said that Gladstone wouldn't admit this.

Friday 27 March. A busy day. Office at 11. Thring,[2] Dr Buchanan,[3] and Peel about the Poisons Bill. At 12 Scotch Committee of Education upon the Heriot Scheme, attended by Duke of Argyll,[4] Rosebery, Baxter,[5] Playfair,[6] and Lord Advocate—

---

[1] Musurus Pasha (1807–91): Turkish minister (1851–6), and Ambassador (1856–85) in London.

[2] Henry Thring (1818–1907), parliamentary draftsman: Counsel to Home Office 1860–9, to Treasury 1869–86; created first Baron Thring by Gladstone, 1886.

[3] Probably Dr George Buchanan (1831–95): principal medical officer, Local Govt. Board, 1879–92; ktd. on retirement.

[4] Eighth Duke of Argyll (1823–1900): Lord Privy Seal 1852–5, 1859–66, 1880–1 (resigned over Irish Land Bill); Indian Sec. 1868–74; finally broke with Gladstone over Home Rule, 1886.

[5] W. E. Baxter (1825–90): M.P. (Lib.) for Montrose burghs 1855–85; minor office 1868–73; senior partner in firm of Dundee merchants, 1870–90; capable administrator and author of several travel books.

[6] Lyon Playfair (1818–98): M.P. (Lib.) 1868–92; P.M.G. 1873–4; Vice-President of Council 1886; cr. Baron 1892.

Mundella and Cumin[1] of course. They approved the scheme,[2] and all went well—a successful idea of my own. Luncheon Athenaeum.

Cabinet at 2. Telegram to Thornton[3] for M. de Giers[4] discussed. Chamberlain pressed for a proposal that the Russians should withdraw from their posts on the debated territory and that we should get the Afghans to withdraw from Penjdeh. If Russia refused, we should have put her in the wrong, have the country and Liberal Party with us, etc. This was postponed until Dufferin sees the Ameer. Trevelyan proposed that the troops should be withdrawn *at once* from Suakim! W. Harcourt would withdraw from Egypt altogether! but Trevelyan's notion was felt to be impossible and was foolish. Then the Lord Advocate came in and we went through the Crofter Land Bill.—The Irish Land Act without Free Sale—a good Bill. Took a good deal of part.

Saturday 28 March. I quite agree with Mrs Carlyle that often the only attainable satisfaction is to feel that you have done all you meant to do—and this I had when I went to bed on Friday night.

Started this morning by 7.15 a.m. train for Euston [for Dundalk, to visit his elder brother, Lord Clermont].

---

[1] Patrick Cumin (1823–90): barrister 1855; editor of *London Review*, 1862; author of a *Manual of Civil Law;* asst. sec., education dept., 1870–84; sec., 1884, on Sandford's retirement, his promotion being forced through by Mundella over Carlingford's head.

[2] George Heriot's Hospital (f. 1624) was enlarged in 1835 to provide free education for poor children, at the instance of Duncan McLaren (1800–86), Edinburgh radical leader. The aim of the Scottish Educational Endowments Commission, set up in 1881, was to alter drastically the regime as set up by McLaren, despite local radical protests. In its report published early in Mar. 1885, the Commission recommended reallocation of endowments under direct State supervision, a curriculum leaning to technical education, and a small governing body in place of the previous corporation of 54 town councillors and ministers. The deputations from the city council that went up to London in Mar. were unable to prevent the scheme coming into effect with little alteration (*Daily Review*, 24 Mar., and *Scotsman*, 28 Mar. 1885).

[3] Sir Edward Thornton (1817–1906), career diplomatist: Ambassador in St Petersburg 1881–5.

[4] N. K. de Giers (1820–95): Russian minister for foreign affairs 1882–95.

Scott,[1] Chargé d'Affaires, Berlin—March 28—Reports conversation with a gentleman who has intimate confidence of Bismarck and exceptional means of knowing political feeling in Russia. The Prince [Bismarck] hopeful that a war between England and Russia may be averted—nothing he more dreaded—had exerted himself earnestly but privately for peace—could not interfere officially. 'Many hotheads and ambitious generals in Russia' but 'no war party such as had forced Alexander II against his will into the Turkish war'. The Czar, Giers, and the Minister for War were all for peace. The Russian ambassador at Berlin does not believe in war.

Wednesday 1 April. . . . I talked about my own situation in office, my feeling at time of unfitness for it etc.—[Clermont] said, as he wrote the other day, that I must not continue in office merely for the income, that I should not lose by it, but should have from him an allowance equal to my official salary, that is £2,000 a year, in addition to the £1,000 which he now gives me. This is very kind, and relieves my mind a good deal.

Saturday 4 April. . . . Cabinet at 12—to consider the Russian answer which had not reached me. Mr G. began by saying that he did not think there could be any difference of opinion as to the character of the answer—It was, he said, a mere insistence upon their own line, their own demands, leaving no room for negotiation, leaving to the Commission the task only of marking out in detail a frontier decided by Russia for herself. This, he said, was treating us as though Russia were a superior dealing with an inferior—This was the general view of the Cabinet,—and it was decided that Granville should send at once for M. de Staal,[2] state to him what the Govt thought of the answer, express incredulity that it could really mean what it seemed to mean, or that this was

---

[1] Charles Stewart Scott (1838–1924), secretary in the British Embassy at Berlin: kt. 1896, P.C. 1898; ended distinguished diplomatic career as Ambassador in St Petersburg, 1898–1904.

[2] Baron de Staal (1822–1907), Russian diplomatist: counsellor of Russian embassy in Constantinople 1864–84; Ambassador in London 1884–1902.

the last word of the Russian Govt. but make no suggestion or counterproposal at present. Which he did and came back to the Cabinet. Staal could do nothing but refer to his Govt. Granville said he, Staal, was very nervous. The only one who opposed this course was Harcourt. He said this was rushing into war and declaimed against it with his violent timidity. He was for holding to the principle of 'the zone' which the Russian answer does not absolutely exclude though it insists on enlarging it, i.e. carrying it farther south towards Herat, and says that such a negotiation after long delay would be useless, would come to nothing. Chamberlain said 'I wish, Harcourt, you would not think it necessary to address us as if we were a bunch of Jingoes' . . .

Sunday 5 April. . . . I have been reading Henry Taylor.[1] It makes me feel how very little of intimate, free, confident, sympathetic friendship I have had or now have—unlike him. It is partly my own fault, partly because my darling woman swallowed up almost all other personal relations, so my isolation now is extraordinary.

Monday 6 April. [Left London for Aix-les-Bains.][2]

Wednesday 8 April. . . . Received Dufferin's very satisfactory telegrams of his conversations with the Ameer,[3] and sent them to the Queen.[4] Ponsonby brought me a very bad one of the attack

[1] Sir Henry Taylor (1800–86), civil servant and poet, whose autobiography appeared in 1885.

[2] Carlingford reached Aix-les-Bains on the morning of 7 Apr., but there is no record of his conversing with the Queen on that day.

[3] Dufferin had seven interviews, 31 Mar.–12 Apr., with the Ameer at Rawalpindi, and by 8 Apr. had sent no less than five optimistic telegrams on their progress to Kimberley, the climax coming on 4 Apr. when the Ameer promised 'to acquiesce in any line we may agree to' (Dufferin's diary, Dufferin MSS. D 1071 H/V/20, ff. 7–9; and telegrams, ibid., H/M1/7, pp. 7–10).

[4] The Queen wrote: 'Had good reports from Lord Dufferin of the meeting of the Ameer with him, at Rawalpindi. The Ameer spoke well and expressed his devotion to England and wish for a continued good understanding, making no difficulties about boundaries—leaving that to us. Lord Carlingford was in high spirits about this, when a telegram arrived, saying that the Russian General, in spite of Emperor's promises, that there should be no hostilities, attacked the Afghans . . .' (*Queen Victoria's Journal*, 8 Apr.)

and taking of Penjdeh[1] by the Russians, after a brave defence by the Afghan garrison. This is outrageous considering the state of our negotiations against Russia.

[At Aix] *Friday 10 April.* From a box sent to me by the Queen:
[1] Sir Ed. Thornton to Lord Granville, April 3, 1885. Principal people here speaking peace—the chief and older military men, even Count Ignatieff.[2] Spoke to M. de Giers yesterday (April 2) about the advance of a Russian column under General Komaroff[3] as mentioned in your telegram. He replied that it was impossible that it could have been with any intention of aggression; (!) he had not heard of the movement, but was convinced that, if it took place, it must have been as a tour of inspection and for the purpose of taking care that no advance should be made by any of the Russian posts. (!) He said that General Komaroff had been expressly instructed to go from Ashkabad to Merv to see personally that there should be no danger of a conflict. (!)
[2] Sir Ed. Thornton to Lord Granville, March 31:
    Great publicity of our military preparations may alarm 'the susceptible nature of the Russians, and they may refuse to listen to reason.' 'As yet however *peace* the mot d'ordre.' 'Strong feeling in favour of war among lower classes, lately imbued with great hatred of all foreigners.' Ignatieff, though he denounces Giers as a coward and traitor to his country, preaches folly of going to war at present—probably still dreams of Constantinople, and thinks Russia should husband her strength for that object—for gaining an outlet from the Black Sea through the Dardanelles, the want of which just now irritates her a good deal. Sir Edward did not know what the Russian answer was. 'Some say it is very stiff and cannot fail to bring about war'—but he cannot believe this.
[3] The Queen to Mr G., April 6, 1885:

---

[1] The Russians under General Komaroff inflicted a heavy defeat on the Afghans at Penjdeh on 30 Mar.

[2] Count N. P. Ignatiev (1832–1908), Russian nationalist and expansionist: negotiated treaty of Peking, 1860, securing much Chinese territory for Russia; Ambassador at Constantinople 1867–78, retiring in disgrace; Minister of the Interior 1881–2.

[3] C.-in-C., Russian forces in central Asia.

'The Queen wishes to express her satisfaction to Mr Gladstone at the firm and proper tone held by the Govt to the Russian ambassador, which she cannot help hoping may have some effect as she thinks the Russians expected the Govt would swallow everything, especially as, whether wrongly or rightly, it is believed that Mr G's views lean towards Russia'. The Queen is certain that we cannot quit the Soudan without leaving some permanent Govt etc. 'The Govt must let the world, beginning with Great Britain, know what our real intentions are, so that precious blood may not have been shed *in vain*, etc.'

[4] Mr Scott, Berlin, to Lord Granville, April 4:

Bismarck's birthday—very much touched by Lord Granville's remembrance—found him 'radiant'. Bismarck much taken aback by the change of Govt in France, relied chiefly on M. Ferry for the 'entente cordiale', had a very high idea of his prudence. If there should be war between Russia and England, Bismarck (Mr Scott thinks) would sacrifice every other interest to his desire to localize it, and would endeavour to secure the neutrality of Turkey. 'He is sensitively anxious to avoid giving Russia any ground of suspicion that he is in *too good relations with England*.' Hence the little notice taken by the German Press of the visit of the P. of Wales. Many of the pro-Russian articles in the *Kölnische Zeitung* believed to be written by Herr von Lindau, who is connected with the Foreign Office, and whose pen is often used by the Prince. Mischief of Blowitz's[1] letters (*The Times*) from Paris.

Saturday 11 April. The Queen sends me a letter to her from Arthur Ellis,[2] from Dublin, written by order of the Prince of

[1] Henri Stefan Opper de Blowitz (1825–1903), foreign correspondent of *The Times:* appointed assistant correspondent in Paris, 1870, on Thiers' recommendation: head of *Times* Paris office, 1875: enabled *Times* to publish Treaty of Berlin before it was even signed: in 1879–89 his influence dominant in *Times* presentation of foreign news: from 1884 Bismarck incensed by his anti-German tendencies: in March 1885 Herbert Bismarck persuaded English ministers to seek to reduce his influence: retired 1903, and wrote highly inaccurate memoirs: a colourful and troublesome person, invited by Acton to contribute a chapter to the *Cambridge Modern History*. See Frank Giles, *A Prince of Journalists* (London, 1963).

[2] Col. Arthur Edward Augustus Ellis (1837–1907): equerry to the Prince of Wales from 1867; K.C.V.O. 1897; serjeant-at-arms in the House of Lords 1898–1901.

Wales.[1] It begins 'Madam' and is addressed to the Countess of Balmoral. 'The Princess of Wales in a green gown, shamrocks in her bonnet.' He has attended the P. of Wales on many public occasions for 19 years, 'and he rarely remembered a better reception than that given yesterday to H.R.H. by the people of Dublin'. The Prince of Wales and his son gratefully received, when they visited the 'slums' of Dublin. 'The evident success of the reception is a great danger to the Nationalists, who feebly do their best to *dénigrer* the whole thing'—April 11, 85.

Sunday 12 April. . . . Left Aix by 4 o'clock train.[2]

Monday 13 April. Drove across to the Nord. Breakfast at a café. Wandered into the church in the Place Lafayette (St. Vincent de Paul) as I have done in old days. Saw the Mass performed, and wondered, when I thought of the narrative in the Gospels.

. . . Train and steamer late, 279 passengers. Several I knew. Obliged to talk to Monk, Coope, and Hall,[3] the Prince of Wales's men. The M.P.s thought war with Russia inevitable.

Tuesday 14 April. This morning found in the papers the death of my old friend Sullivan,[4] the Irish Chancellor. Very sudden indeed. I regret him very much—he was a fine fellow, able, courageous,

---

[1] The Prince and Princess of Wales and Prince Albert Victor left London for a tour of Ireland on 7 Apr., visiting Dublin, Cork, and Belfast, and returning on 27 Apr.

[2] Though Carlingford dined with the Queen and her ladies on 10 and 11 Apr., her *Journal* contains no report of his conversation on this visit save that given above for 8 Apr.

[3] Probably Charles James Monk (1824–1900), barrister and director of Suez Canal Co.: M.P. (Lib.) Gloucester City 1859, 1865–85, 1895–1900; Octavius Edward Coope (1814–86), partner in Ind Coope's brewery: M.P. (Cons.) Yarmouth 1847–8, Middlesex 1874–85, Brentford 1885–6; and Charles Hall (1843–1900): Att.-Gen. to the Prince of Wales 1877–92; not an M.P. at this time, but M.P. (Cons.), Chesterton 1885–92, Holborn 1892–1900.

[4] Sir Edward Sullivan, Bt. (1822–85): M.P. (Lib.) Mallow 1865–70; Att.-Gen. for Ireland 1868–70; Lord Chancellor of Ireland from 11 Dec. 1883 to his death, 13 Apr. 1885; see below, p. 89, n. 1.

warmhearted, sincere,—a true friend of mine and of my darling's, who knew well what he was and liked him very much. She never forgot his refusal to come to the Cabinet to explain the draft Land Bill in Nov. '69, (when Gladstone asked him to do so) saying that Mr Fortescue had done it all.[1]

... Cabinet at 2. Before it began Northbrook told me that Hartington was likely to resign, (perhaps Childers), not on the question of giving up the Khartoum expedition, but of announcing it now—.

Mr G. came in late, evidently after negotiations with Hartington, and proposed to postpone the decision about the Soudan to next day, saying that he had great hope of agreement. He was very benign, and showed a kind of senile cheerfulness which I had never noticed in him so much. After this there was a good deal of conversation but nothing really to do. The idea of abandoning the Khartoum expedition has ripened rapidly under the pressure of a very possible Russian war . . .

Wednesday 15 April. Cabinet again at 2.30. Luncheon at Athenaeum with Goschen.[2]

At Cabinet Mr G. read substance of statement that he proposed to make to House on the Vote of Credit—great part of it written by Hartington. Hartington read a telegram from Wolseley protesting against abandonment of Dongola, if the Khartoum plan is given up.

[1] For an opposite view, see Kimberley's journal, 31 Oct. 1869, 'Now having heard Sullivan, the Irish Attorney General, expound his scheme, I see light. It is evident that Sullivan, who is a very able man, the ablest Irishman I have known, is the real author of the plan. Chichester Fortescue shows much less mastery of the subject' (E. Drus, op. cit., p. 9). Kimberley was however very much out to disparage Fortescue in 1868–74, because of their earlier quarrel in 1865–6 over the question of Fortescue's promotion to the Cabinet which Kimberley had strenuously and successfully opposed.

[2] G. J. Goschen (1831–1907), very moderate Liberal, becoming a Conservative 1887: M.P. (Lib.) 1863–86, (Cons.) 1887–1900; Chancellor of the Duchy of Lancaster 1866; president of Poor Law Board 1868–71; First Lord of the Admiralty 1871–4, 1895–1900; appointed Ambassador in Constantinople 1880–1 after Carlingford had reluctantly accepted that office; Chancellor of the Exchequer 1887–1892; cr. Viscount 1900; declined to form a Coalition government in defence of the Union, Jan. 1886.

Surprised to find Lord Selborne[1] at the Cabinet—his wife buried yesterday. What can one think of this?

Thursday 16 April. Board at South Kensington, 11 to 1. Mundella not there, which certainly makes it more agreeable.

Friday 17 April. [Carlingford took steps to sell a portrait of the Waldegrave family by Sir Joshua Reynolds.] . . . This is the right, the wise, the necessary thing to do, if I am to do the best for the estate, work the new seams of coal etc. (and nothing interests me so much.)[2]

. . . Wrote to the Queen, in a great hurry to catch F.O. messenger. Tried to soothe her about abandonment of Khartoum expedition.[3]

Saturday 18 April. Found four circulation boxes waiting for me at dinner time—one contained a letter[4] from M. de Giers to Staal, sent by latter to Granville, with Granville's draft of reply, a very good one. The tone and line of Giers very bad. Another box con-

---

[1] Lady Selborne had died on 10 Apr. and Selborne had missed the previous two Cabinets.

[2] After much anxious inquiry, Carlingford finally placed the picture in the hands of Christie's in Nov. (Carlingford to Clermont, 20 Nov. 1885; Strachie MSS.)

[3] Carlingford's letter to the Queen of 17 Apr. (Royal Archives B/36/44) provides the clearest statement of his views on the Sudan: '. . . Lord Carlingford writes entirely from his own point of view, and without communication with others. He had thought for some time that an expedition to Khartoum would prove to be intolerable, that the object to be gained (now that poor General Gordon is gone) would not be sufficient to justify it, and that public opinion would not permit it—but he did not know until he returned to London how rapidly the idea of abandoning that plan had ripened under the pressure of a great war very possibly approaching . . . Lord Carlingford cannot answer for Lord Wolseley's views,—but he has certainly found out how immensely he at first underrated the difficulties of the expedition, when he said that he might be able to get to Khartoum before the hot season, and named a day for taking Berber. Now he says that a Khartoum expedition would probably occupy two years.' Carlingford also described the adoption of a forward policy in early February, to which he had not then objected, as 'a rash decision'.

[4] See below (p. 145) under 'Miscellaneous Jottings', no. 4, for terms of the letter.

tained telegrams on the subject of Freycinet's[1] violent treatment of the Egyptian Govt about the suppression of the *Bosphore Egyptien*[2] —which looks like an awkward and serious affair. Such is the state of foreign affairs! Lord Granville asked one of the Rothschilds (?) what sort of man Freycinet was, and the answer was 'Fancy Sir Edward Watkin[3] Foreign Secretary!'

Dined at home—Read a secret paper signed by Major Rothwell, Intelligence Branch of War Office, headed *England's Means of Offence against Russia*.[4] It takes a most hopeless view. Nothing to be done in Baltic—nothing in Black Sea, except at Batoum— etc. etc.

Sunday 19 April. . . . Circulation box come with request from Granville and Hartington that the paper on our means of offence against Russia should be returned or destroyed. Sent mine back— and it had come in an envelope!

Monday 20 April. . . . Cabinet at 2—The Vote of Credit and the Budget. Vote of Credit to be £11,000,000—Normal deficit for 1885–6 £4,000,000 = £15,000,000.—Childers proposed to take part of this sum out of the 6 or 7 millions now devoted to payment of debt during the next three years and to make up the rest by the increase of the Death Duties on real property, and by raising the duties on spirits and beer. This proposal was very roughly handled—Harcourt, Dilke, and Chamberlain protesting, on party grounds, against increasing the working man's taxes, with the general election and the new voters before us—long talk— question adjourned.[5]

Tuesday 21 April. Office. Cabinet. Budget discussed again, and

---

[1] C. de S. de Freycinet (1828–1923), French Premier 1879, Jan.–July 1882, 1886, 1890: Foreign Minister, Jan.–Apr. 1882, 1885.

[2] An Egyptian newspaper so hostile to British interests that the authorities had suppressed it on 8 Apr. 1885. The French protest which arrived in Cairo on 16 Apr. was a crude attempt to exploit the difficulties of the British government at a time of acute crisis in Anglo-Russian relations.

[3] A railway magnate from Manchester and the epitome of a self-made man.

[4] A copy of this is in the Public Record Office: CAB 37/13/36.

[5] See also account of this Cabinet under 7 May below.

again adjourned. Mr. G. said he could not reconcile himself to laying all the fresh taxation on Income Tax and Death Duties, no part of it on Indirect Taxation. Two telegrams from Giers—very unsatisfactory—very confused, perplexed, and heated conversation which produced nothing. Harcourt talked long and loud, interrupted everybody, declared violently for giving way in everything. Kimberley grew, very naturally, angry. Chamberlain said he preached the doctrine of 'eating dirt' 'offensively'. When W. Harcourt demanded what others would do—what they had to propose? Hartington said 'You seem to think we ought to be ready with a proposal offhand—but that is not so easy—*Your* way is easy enough—to give way in everything.' W. Harcourt said if Russia attacked Herat he would go to war with her. Chamberlain at our end of the table, 'He'd find some way out of that when the time came.' At the House of Lords in the Tea Room had a talk with Northbrook and Kimberley about what could be done. (Northbrook said, now that Harcourt's not here, we can talk rationally.) Kimberley started the idea that we should propose to Russia to get the Penjdeh incident out of the way of the frontier negotiation by referring it to a third power. Northbrook and I liked this.

Wednesday 22 April. . . . Wrote letters at home until 2.30, principally on Essex Lieutenancy[1] business.

Friday 24 April. . . . Office and House. Talk with Mundella about the directorship of the Edinburgh Museum, the Medical Bill, etc. etc. His touchiness and vanity require management. He began to storm in an absurd way about question of dissolving a School Board, and cooled down rapidly, when I pointed out difficulties.

. . . Most important drafts came round embodying the idea of proposing to Russia to refer the question of the Penjdeh affair to the judgement of the Head of a friendly State. Granville told me that this was objected to by Harcourt, and also by Hartington

---

[1] Carlingford was Lord-Lieutenant of Essex 1873–92.

and Rosebery, but on opposite grounds[1]—the latter objecting *unless* the Cabinet made up its mind to withdraw our Ambassador, if this overture were refused! Some of them went to discuss with Mr G. but it was not a Cabinet, and I was not asked to go. It is a most critical question—but I see nothing better.

Saturday 25 April. . . . Cabinet at 12. Mr G. began by announcing that Dilke and Chamberlain had consented to waive their strong objections to an increase of duty on spirits and beer (or any new taxation on the working classes) and he thanked them for it.

Then came the *Bosphore* affair which lasted long, and H. James and Herschell[2] came in, they clearly of opinion that the method of suppressing the paper by closing the printing office was illegal. Decided that the office must be reopened, and that an apology must be made by Nubar[3] and by this Govt—but the paper should not be allowed to reappear, and the officers should not be punished.

Chamberlain's proposal—à propos of Freycinet's outrageous conduct in dealing with the case of the *Bosphore Egyptien*, with-holding the Financial Convention from the Chambers, etc., he proposed that we should take this opportunity of getting out of Egypt altogether, should tell France that we found our position intolerable, that we would no longer act for Europe in that country, would give up the Convention and the loan, let Egypt be bankrupt, and come away as soon as possible, only insisting on the freedom of the Suez Canal. This strange proposal (made I suppose for future use) was not supported by anybody, not even by Dilke or W. Harcourt. Granville and then Mr G. said that to do this now would be to allow ourselves to be driven out of Egypt by France—and besides, however bad and unfriendly the conduct of France, we have been in the wrong in the case of the *Bosphore*. The matter then dropped, except that W. Harcourt and others said that Bismarck's hand was in this act of France—which Rosebery did not believe.

[1] This means Hartington and Rosebery were of one mind as against Harcourt (see below, 25 Apr.).

[2] Attorney-General and Solicitor-General, respectively.

[3] Nubar Pasha (1825–99): Egyptian Foreign Minister 1866–78; Premier 1878–9, 1884–8, 1894–5.

Then talk about the Vote of Credit debate. Telegram came from Lumsden increasing the proof of unprovoked character of Komaroff's outrage.[1] Mr G. said that he had a letter from Stead[2] editor of the *Pall Mall* which he had answered shortly 'regretting that he did not give that support to the Govt of the country which might be expected from every good citizen under existing circumstances'. Rosebery asked about the draft to Staal. It has gone, after wrangle between Harcourt and Kimberley—the words 'as a final effort to preserve friendly relations' being modified to please Harcourt—'final' left out.[3]

Dined at Gloucester House—sat between Granville and Hartington—a great deal of talk—Granville said that our French communication would probably succeed, our Russian one would *not*. Staal had said he 'was afraid it wouldn't do'. Hartington longing to escape from office[4]—had been against the proposal now made to Russia believing it to be useless—would have withdrawn our Ambassador at once—*that* must follow, if our proposal refused.—He held that Mr G. had given a great and needless importance to the arrangement with Russia against either party advancing, the breach of which at Pul-i-Khisti and Penjdeh now constitutes the great danger.

Monday 27 April. . . . I have had hardly any Irish work so far this year—This is a relief, but on the other hand combined with the great and engrossing foreign questions, it makes my official position much more insignificant than it was in '81–84. It is a

---

[1] Lumsden's tel. of 21 Apr. quoted a letter from Komaroff to the Afghan commander, announcing his intention to attack (Kimberley to Dufferin, 25 Apr.: Dufferin MSS. D 1071 H/M1/7, pp. 24–5).

[2] W. T. Stead (1849–1912), journalist: prominent in Bulgarian atrocities agitation; asst. ed. (under John Morley) of *Pall Mall Gazette*, 1880–3; its editor, 1883–90; founded *Review of Reviews*, 1890; because of his Russian sympathies, believed by Kimberley to be 'entirely in the hands of Madame de Novikoff and M. Lessar. No doubt money as well as "facts" and arguments are freely supplied' (Kimberley to Dufferin, 27 Mar. 1885, Dufferin MSS. D 1071 H/M1/3, p. 42).

[3] After the Cabinet two notes were sent to the Russian Ambassador, one proposing an inquiry into the Penjdeh incident, the other suggesting an international arbitration on the boundary (Kimberley to Dufferin, 25 Apr., ibid., D 1071 H/M1/7, pp. 23–4).

[4] Cf. his vote for resignation, 28 Feb.

comfort to me that my wise loving darling foresaw the probability of my being offered the Privy Seal in that coming Liberal Govt of which we used to talk and which she was never to see, and said I ought to take it.

Tuesday 28 April. . . . Cabinet at 2—very nervous and feeling unfit but took a good deal of part—Principal Bills considered— Princess Beatrice's Bill (question of Committee on general subject of provision for Royal Family), Crofters' Bill, *Crimes Bill* —The organized obstruction by the Irish has begun already upon the estimates—From the moment that a Crimes Bill is announced they will obstruct everything—*Spencer said*[1] *the renewal of great part of the Crimes Bill was necessary.* He wished also for a Land Purchase Bill, a Local Govt Bill, and an announcement of aboli- tion of the Lord-Lieutenancy and a Royal Residence. Mr G. held that a large Local Govt Bill was closely connected with a Crimes Bill and a Land Purchase Bill, and that all must go together. Chamberlain said he could not be party to a Crimes Bill, unless there were a very large Local Govt Bill—that it would be im- possible to carry a Crimes Bill alone, etc. I said a Crimes Bill was absolutely necessary in any case, that I was in favour of a broad and liberal Local Govt Bill, in the sense understood in England, i.e. *County* Govt—a Committee[2] appointed. Scotch Secretary Bill discussed. Rosebery to bring it in in the House of Lords— *Scotch Education* to be included, but not made a vital point. I said this could not be justified on educational grounds, which was not denied—it is only 'Home Rule'.

Wednesday 29 April. Irish Committee on the Crimes Bill, at 2, at Campbell-Bannerman's[3] room at House of Commons. There,

[1] Cf. his conversation with Carlingford on 22 Feb., above. Spencer's Irish programme put before the Cabinet on 28 Apr. was the same in its main headings as that he had outlined in a Cabinet memorandum dated 25 Mar. (B.M. Add. MS. 44312, ff. 38–43). The Cabinet of 28 Apr. was the first meeting of the year at which Irish business was considered.

[2] Subsequently referred to as the Irish Committee.

[3] Henry Campbell-Bannerman (1836–1908): M.P. 1868–1908; minor office 1871–4, 1880–4; Irish Secretary 1884–5, outside Cabinet; Sec. for war 1886, 1892–5; Liberal leader, 1898–1908; Prime Minister 1905–8.

Spencer, Trevelyan, Chamberlain, W. Harcourt, Bannerman. W. Harcourt protested against dropping any section of the present Act.[1] Chamberlain against any Crimes Bill at all! Then we went through the clauses, and by a majority accepted Spencer's proposals, to drop certain parts of the Act, which he held to be unnecessary or to do more harm than good, and to renew the rest.

Spencer gave me a great 'Local Govt' plan of Chamberlain's to read.[2] He and Chamberlain had been with Mr G. for a long time. Chamberlain would hardly consent to come to the Committee. *Mr G. very favourable to his plan.* Spencer greatly annoyed with Trevelyan, who had told him he was entirely with him, and today said that 'he almost entirely agreed with Chamberlain'. . . . Read and made extracts from the 'Scheme' given to Spencer by Chamberlain, which proposes a great elective 'Central Board' in Dublin!

Thursday 30 April. . . . I had returned the Scheme to Spencer with a letter saying that it filled me with astonishment that any serious politician could take it up—Talk with Spencer in the House of Lords—Chamberlain received the scheme from Parnell[3] through

[1] See his reported statement in the same vein (22 Feb., above).

[2] Chamberlain had sent various documents sketching a Central Board scheme to Spencer, but the one mentioned here is probably that written by Chamberlain on 25 Apr., just after his interview with Manning, and sent to the Archbishop as well as to certain ministers (for text, see *Irish Historical Studies*, viii. 255-7). Spencer replied from Dublin, 26 Apr., disapproving of the Central Board scheme, except perhaps for educational matters only, though he did not finally commit himself (printed, ibid., pp. 257-9).

[3] This is misleading. Chamberlain had been in direct negotiation (Nov. 1884–Feb. 1885) with Parnell through O'Shea over a Central Board scheme, while simultaneously engaged in indirect soundings of nationalist opinion on the same issue through a Walsall solicitor, W. H. Duignan. Both sets of negotiations had lapsed, Jan./Feb. 1885. By Apr., they belonged to the past, and only mattered insofar as they had given Chamberlain an idea of the range of possibilities. Chamberlain's proposals in Mar. and Apr. were much more the product of his discussions with Spencer and with Manning, than of his shadowy links with Parnell via O'Shea. Chamberlain's plan, far from originating with Parnell, was passed by Manning to Parnell, who showed no enthusiasm. See C. H. D. Howard, 'Joseph Chamberlain, Parnell, and the Irish "Central Board" Scheme, 1884-5', *Irish Historical Studies*, viii (Sept. 1953): and his 'Documents relating to the Irish "Central Board" Scheme, 1884-5', ibid. viii (Mar.1953).

O'Shea[1]—just as he did the Kilmainham proposals. Cardinal Manning has come[2] to Chamberlain to support the plan—It is a most serious state of things.

Spencer told me that Courtenay Boyle[3] was obliged to leave him, did not know what he should do without him—asked me to let him have Dasent. I felt bound not to refuse. The question of a Private Secretary being so much more important for him than for me—but I hate it, Dasent being a great comfort, and his loss great.

Derby and Kimberley had heard of Chamberlain's proposals, and do not like them—Derby said it would probably break up the Govt.

Friday 1 May. Walked up from House of Lords with Derby, who was anxious to know about Chamberlain's scheme.

The Irish Committee at Spencer House at 11. There—Spencer, Chamberlain, Hartington, Harcourt, Trevelyan, Childers, Lefevre, Campbell-Bannerman, and self. We sat till 2.30—it was most unsatisfactory—no discussion of a County Govt Bill.

Chamberlain at once stated his scheme, and the origin of it. It had been long in his mind. He had lately found that Parnell had a similar plan, which he said would content him and most Home

---

[1] Capt. William Henry O'Shea (1840–1905), political intermediary and intriguer: officer in Hussars, 1858–62; M.P. (Home Ruler) for Clare, 1880–5; for Galway, Feb.–June 1886 (as Parnell's personal nominee; did not vote for Home Rule Bill, 1886, or join the Parnellite party); befriended by Parnell, 1881; agent of Chamberlain and Herbert Gladstone in Kilmainham Treaty negotiations, 1882; employed by Chamberlain 1884–5 to involve Parnell in radical Irish policy, especially Central Board scheme; blamed by Chamberlain for failure of radical-Irish entente, but continued to hope for Irish Secretaryship in a Chamberlain government (Chamberlain MSS. contain 176 letters to or from O'Shea); employed by Churchill, 1886–7, in his second abortive attempt to settle Irish education questions in alliance with the bishops; constantly attacked by Parnell after 1886; revenged himself by bringing divorce action against his wife, 1890.

[2] In fact it was Chamberlain who, on 24 Apr., had called on Manning, for what was probably their only interview in the period of the Central Board negotiations.

[3] G. Courtney Boyle (1845–1901), civil servant, a gt.-nephew of 8th Earl of Cork: educ. Eton and Ch.Ch., Oxford; m. d. of 1st Earl of Cawdor; Spencer's private sec. 1868–73, 1882–5; asst. sec., Local Govt. Board., 1885–6; asst. sec., Bd. of Trade, 1886–93; perm. sec., Board. of Trade, 1893; K.C.B. 1892.

Rulers!? (The other day Parnell in a speech[1] in Ireland said that 'Grattan's Parliament' was the least they could demand)—that Cardinal Manning promised that it would secure the support of the Church—he was himself convinced that it was the only way of avoiding Home Rule. Spencer, Harcourt, and I declared against such a scheme. Childers, Trevelyan, Lefevre for it. Hartington said little, but was evidently against. Bannerman said nothing. I said I considered it 'throwing up the cards', a virtual acceptance of Home Rule, and in the worst form—putting the central control of almost all Irish administration into the hands of an elected Assembly, ousting the Crown and its Ministers etc. W. Harcourt, very absurdly, saw no objection to this, *but would not create a Central Board, because it would be used for ulterior purposes.* The Committee was divided, without chance of agreement.

Monday 4 May. . . . Office and House. Granville made a statement about the *Bosphore*,[2] and about Russia—agreement arrived at to refer the question of the 'Penjdeh incident' and 'the agreement of March 16' to the head of a friendly state—the frontier negotiations to go on. Salisbury catechised Granville, but got no more out of him.

Read at Athenaeum, article in *Deutsche Rundschau* on Darwinism and Ethics, and Caird on Comte.

. . . [Lord] Sydney has been and looks very ill.

Tuesday 5 May. . . . I have heard nothing of what is going on about the Crimes Bill etc.—not a word from Spencer, who has only appeared for a few moments at the House, and has given me the impression of avoiding me. With Mr G. as usual, I have no communication at all.

The books which I have in my bedroom and which I read more

[1] According to Palmer's *Index to the Times*, Parnell made no outdoor speeches between the end of Jan. and 7 May 1885. Carlingford may have had in mind the famous speech at Cork, 21 Jan. 1885, which was certainly a snub to any central board scheme.

[2] He announced that the Egyptian and British governments had allowed the paper to reopen and apologized to the French, having discovered that they had no right to suppress it in the first place. See *Hansard*, vol. 297, cols. 1470–4.

or less at night or before getting up are at this moment George Sand's *Histoire de Ma Vie*, Balzac's *Père Goriot*, and Croker.

Thursday 7 May. There was a Cabinet. I think this was the Cabinet at which Childers stated his deficit and his Budget.[1] (I am writing on May 20.) Eleven millions to be found, between 'normal' deficit and Vote of Credit. Childers proposed to find it 1) by suspension of repayment of debt 2) by increase of Income Tax 3) by increase of the Death Duties on real property 4) by increase of the Beer and Spirit Duties. To this last there was strong opposition from Chamberlain, Dilke and Harcourt, on account of the General Election, and the new voters. Others, Derby etc, insisted with Childers on the necessity of putting some part of the new taxes on the payers of indirect taxation—the working classes— and this was evidently Mr G's view.

The question was left open but at a subsequent Cabinet [in fact the Cabinet held on 25 April] Mr G. announced that the opponents of the Beer and Spirits Duties had consented to the proposal, and he thanked them very much for it.

[The whole of the entry for 7 May above is lightly crossed out in the diary, with a note by Carlingford explaining that he had misdated the Cabinets described above. The discussion reported here in fact refers to Childers' budget, first considered in cabinet on 20 April.]

Saturday 9 May. ... Breakfast[2] (the Club) at Goschen's—... Walked home with Trevelyan—he thought the Govt would hold together. A Cabinet called unexpectedly to settle what announcement should be made as to the Soudan. The difficulty with the Chancellor and Northbrook, who had threatened to resign, settled by giving a good deal of jaw [*sic*] as to the time of evacuating the Province of Dongola—. Kimberley stated the points of the

[1] The budget was discussed mainly at the Cabinets of 20 and 21 Apr.

[2] The Breakfast Club consisted of about a dozen members who, during the season, entertained each other once a week in their own houses. Its members linked Whig politics and Whig literary culture, and included Acton, Lansdowne, Goschen, Aberdare, Dufferin, Erskine May, and Courtney. See Sir George Leveson Gower, *Years of Content 1858–1886* (London, 1940), pp. 174–5.

frontier upon which he had agreed with M. (Lassar?).[1] Approved by Dufferin and his Council unanimously. Then Mr G. said the announcement of Irish Bills must be made very soon. Derby and Kimberley wished to know what proposals had been considered by the Committee of Cabinet. Chamberlain then stated his 'Local Govt' scheme, as he had done at Spencer House, saying that without it he could not be a party to a Crimes Bill.

Harcourt and Dilke had left the room before this came on, and Trevelyan went away after it had begun! Derby declared against Chamberlain's scheme, then I did the same absolutely. I said that, taking it as it stood upon paper, the 'Central Board' would be a thoroughly bad form of Govt, would completely overshadow the Executive etc—but that it would be inevitably used to gain more power for the object of separation etc. (The Chancellor agreed with what I said.) Then Spencer strongly against—'it would be a *Convention* sitting in Dublin'. Kimberley ditto. Childers and Lefevre supported Chamberlain. Mr G. was *with* him—'only hope for Ireland' etc but would not go into the argument—'quite useless'—. . .

Sunday 10 May. . . . During this day I thought of myself *as out* of office, and thought of my future in that belief. I felt a sense of freedom and relief, though I asked myself—How shall I use this desolate life? How shall I do without the necessities of official life, which are not only chains and pains but also support and protection? Mr. G at the end of the Cabinet evidently thought the Govt at an end.

Monday 11 May. Found the children in the garden . . . most unwilling to come back to London. Went to the Levée. Harcourt took me aside, and scattered by a word my Dudbrook[2] dreams. He said he had spent Sunday in negotiating between Spencer and Chamberlain, and had brought them to a compromise—Chamberlain gives up his 'Local Govt' scheme and engages not to raise the

---

[1] M. Lessar was minister at the Russian embassy in London, under M. de Staal, the Ambassador.

[2] Carlingford's Essex estate, which he sold shortly before his death in 1898, probably because of financial difficulties.

question until after the elections—Spencer gives up the *Meetings* and *Search* sections of the Crimes Act. *W. Harcourt dwelt upon the danger of Gladstone out of office 'throwing his shield over Parnell, Chamberlain, Dilke, etc.' against Hartington and his friends.* Harcourt is an extraordinary fellow—the other day he was the first and loudest to say that the Govt could not go on—that the best thing that could happen was that we should find or make an opportunity to resign. He never attempts to excuse or reconcile his violent changes of opinion. Spencer told me the same story at the House of Lords.

My feeling was one of deep disappointment and depression. A speech of the Duke of Argyll on Russia was stopped by a scream from Lord Dormer,[1] who had fallen back in an epileptic fit. The House adjourned.

Tuesday 12 May. Very despondent this morning, and in the night, when I lay awake. I feel as if I could not go on playing my part—small one as it is—in public life. To a meeting of Irish Committee at Spencer House—there, Spencer, Campbell Bannerman, Walker[2] (Irish Solicitor General), Chamberlain, Harcourt, Trevelyan. We went through the surviving sections of the Crimes Act without much difficulty, and all seemed settled, when Chamberlain raised the question of *time*. He had told Harcourt, when Spencer had consented to the Bill being cut down, as now intended, *that he thought it might stand without limit of time*, as a measure not exceptional. Since then he had consulted others, *Dilke, John Morley,* Jesse Collings,[3] etc, and *found that he could only consent to it if limited to one year*. He said that Mr. G. did not agree with him about this. Upon this Spencer and Harcourt protested

---

[1] Cf. Rosebery's journal, 11 May: '. . . while the Duke of Argyll was perorating, a hideous scream like that of a cat on the tiles was heard, repeated more than once . . .' Dormer, the 11th Baron, recovered and lived on till 1900 when he succumbed to angina.

[2] Samuel Walker, Q.C., (1832–1911), Irish law officer: Irish bar 1855; Q.C. 1872; Sol.-Gen. for Ireland 1883–5; Att.-Gen. for Ireland 1885, 1886; M.P. Londonderry 1884–5; Lord Chancellor of Ireland 1892–5; Lord Justice of Appeal 1895–1905.

[3] Jesse Collings (1831–1920), Chamberlain's closest henchman: M.P. 1880–1918.

strongly—it had not been part of the bargain, but the *permanence* of the new Bill had greatly weighed with Spencer in making his concessions—In answer to some pressure from me, Chamberlain said 'I won't break with my party whatever happens', but he told Spencer that in return for one year, he would withdraw his opposition to the Clauses which Spencer had given up.

Spencer refused the one year and the whole question was again unsettled. Office and House. Dined with the Aberdeens.[1]

Wednesday 13 May. Wrote letters until luncheon. Office—then to a meeting of the Governors of Charterhouse School.

Thursday 14 May. To Board at South Kensington—Walked away with Mundella, who talks in a very discontented way. . . . Paid a visit to John Wilson the bookseller, and had a very interesting talk on the great subjects which was a relief to me, it is so seldom that I can speak freely of these things.

Friday 15 May. (Cabinet at 2.) In consequence of a note from Spencer, went to Devonshire House at 11. At Mr G's desire he had called together those members of the Cabinet who agreed with him about the Crimes Act, Granville, Derby, Northbrook, Kimberley, Rosebery, myself, Hartington of course.—Mr G. had proposed a compromise with Chamberlain, that the Bill should be for 2 years, which Chamberlain and Dilke accepted, on the understanding that if the Radicals insisted on 1 year, they would resign, wouldn't fight against one year. We were all in great difficulty, Spencer of course especially, who has been hardly used, and has got himself into a hole, having made concessions (in hope of a permanent Bill) from which he cannot now escape—the one thing that turned the scale in favour of acceptance of the above and against resignation was the great mischief (if the Govt

---

[1] 7th Earl (1847–1934) and Countess (1857–1939) of Aberdeen, later 1st Marquess and Marchioness. The Earl began life as a Conservative but joined the Liberals in 1879 in protest against Disraeli's foreign policy; was Ld.-Lt. of Ireland Feb.–July 1886, 1905–15, and Gov.-Gen. of Canada 1893–8. She was the sister of a future Liberal chief whip, Tweedmouth, and the real politician in the family. In 1885–6 Gladstone was a frequent visitor to Dollis Hill, their house near London.

broke up upon this) of having Chamberlain, Dilke, etc with Parnell & Co., under Gladstone's aegis, arrayed against Harting-ton and the moderate Liberals. It was also said with great force especially by Hartington that it was most important to have Chamberlain and Dilke committed to a Crimes Bill, however much reduced. I gave my opinion this way telling Spencer at the same time that I was quite ready to resign with him. At last Spencer decided not to resign.

Cabinet—to settle Mr G's announcement of Bills for same day. New difference (they are endless!) arose upon the Purchase Bill. Mr G. was willing only for Spencer's sake, but Dilke said he and Chamberlain would resign and it was given up!

A Purchase Bill without guarantee had been apparently agreed to by the Cabinet, and had been accepted by Mr G., who was discussing only the number of millions to be mentioned, when Dilke interposed, said that the differences between Chamberlain and himself, and the rest of the Cabinet, were so deep, this Purchase question a new proof of them—that it would be better that they should retire. (This was said after a conversation on paper between himself and Chamberlain which goes on constantly.) Upon this Harcourt threw over Spencer at once, and said that Purchase must be given up. He objurgated me because I was indignant that Spencer and the Prime Minister and the rest of us should be coerced to give up such a measure as Land Purchase, merely because Chamberlain and Dilke wanted to reserve it for the new Parliament in order that it might help their Home Rule schemes. Spencer said he was quite entitled to resign though he would not do so. Purchase was given up. Trevelyan absent.

Saturday 16 May. Cabinet[1] at 12. The Budget again. Childers—looking very ill—stated the amendments he proposed in his Budget. Wine duties to be raised, the negotiation with Spain

---

[1] Gladstone's letter to the Queen reporting on the discussions of this Cabinet Council is in the Cabinet Papers in the Public Record Office, but has been bound in the wrong volume, that for 1886. The exact reference is P.R.O. CAB 41/20/19, dated 16 May (which in 1886 would have fallen on a Sunday, a most unlikely day for a Cabinet). The context also makes it clear that it belongs to 1885, not 1886.

(Morier's)[1] having broken down. (He found great fault with Morier.) The increase of the Beer and Spirit duties to be reduced. W. Harcourt denounced it all—no use discussing it etc—impossible to carry it now that there was to be no war. Chamberlain and Dilke took same line—fatal budget for the elections etc. Mr G. and the Cabinet generally were for postponing the question, impossible to announce as yet that we need not prepare for war. Childers said he must *resign*—everyone remonstrated—He was wrongheaded and foolish about it, as there was no decision upon his proposals, and resignation would have been quite premature— I told him he would not be able to explain it to any audience.

Wrote to him afterwards.[2]

Monday 18 May. . . . Debate upon the Soudan brought on by Wemyss.[3] The Duke of Argyll made an elaborate speech, eloquent and foolish, reproaching the Govt. for having shrunk from the task of holding and civilizing the Soudan. Characteristic of the want of common sense and sound judgement which accompanies his gifts and attainments. It is this, as Granville said to me, that explains his utter want of influence in Scotland. Salisbury said the most unpleasant things of the Govt, but would not vote with Wemyss for the completion of the Suakin-Berber railway. Wentworth gave the Govt great credit for leaving the Soudan, and made a speech of some interest, full of admiration for the Arabs.

Tuesday 19 May. Council at Windsor. . . . Thought Mr G. looking old and feebler. He had been unusually irritable in the

[1] Sir Robert Morier (1826–93), career diplomat: held posts in minor European capitals 1866–81; Ambassador at Madrid 1881–5, at St Petersburg 1885–93. Carlingford had been best man at his wedding in 1861.

[2] This letter has not survived in the Childers MSS.

[3] 10th Earl of Wemyss (1818–1914): M.P. 1841–6, 1847–83; as Lord Elcho was prominent in fomenting Liberal opposition to 1866 Reform Bill; succ. his father as peer, 1883; held extreme views on individualism. His motion, which was eventually withdrawn without a division, called on the Government to retain the Eastern Sudan for an unspecified period when the rest of the country was evacuated (*Hansard*, vol. 298, col. 655). Although Salisbury took a slightly different line in debate, Wemyss was in fact acting with his full approval. (Henry Manners to Salisbury, 17 May 1885, Salisbury MSS.)

House of Commons on Monday—worried by the Opposition and not well, Lord Granville said. Saw the Queen for some time—very much annoyed and indignant about the abandonment of the Soudan, especially of Dongola: as to the latter, I am not surprised at her feelings. She talked of Mr G., and said the best thing he could do would be to go to the Lords.

Thursday 21 May. . . . Received Ripon[1] at the office to discuss certain cases of R. Catholic schools, to which we refused grants. Mundella and Cumin were with me, and Mundella harangued in his somewhat exasperating fashion, with '*I* have done this', '*I* wouldn't do that' etc.

Ripon went to the room that was the Lord President's until the Home Secretary moved to the new Home Office. Being in the Education Dept. and close to the Vice-President, I have no doubt that it led to more frequent communication between the two, and that the change has increased the independence of the Vice-President.

House of Lords. Talked to Kimberley and Northbrook of the present condition of our foreign affairs, which is deplorable. France bullying us about the *Bosphore*, Germany and France about the tax on the Egyptian coupons, the Egyptian Convention not ratified at Paris or anywhere, etc. They entirely agreed, especially Northbrook. There has been another difficulty with Chamberlain and Dilke about Irish land purchase. Mr G., under pressure from the Ulster and other Liberal members, announced a Bill, having before announced no Bill. Chamberlain and Dilke resigned or threatened to resign, but it has been got over somehow. We had an informal meeting of Cabinet in Mr G's room, House of Commons—about the Russian negotiations which do not advance.

Saturday 23 May. . . . The Cabinet works in a glass house. The differences about the Crimes Bill and Local Govt and Purchase in Ireland, and the line taken by Chamberlain and Dilke, are

---

[1] Ripon had become a Catholic in 1874.

faithfully reported in a Birmingham paper,[1] upon which the *Pall Mall* comments.

My eyes trouble me—painful after reading.

Tuesday 26 May. Left Dudbrook early—a good deal to do in London. . . . Said goodbye to Dasent, and saw young Peel who is to act as my P.S.—good looking fellow—Perhaps I have been weak in letting Spencer have Dasent, but the work there is far more important than mine, and it is good for himself.

Wednesday 27 May. [At Balmoral.] . . . Henry Ponsonby came to see me, said the Queen was anxious to tell me about a long letter she had had from Mr G. upon Irish policy. Dined with Her Majesty . . . The Queen talked a good deal after dinner. To bed as soon as I could. Very low.

Thursday 28 May. The Queen has sent me Mr Gladstone's long letter, of which she spoke last night. It is a most remarkable and important statement of views upon Ireland. It does not reveal whether or not the writer expects or intends to take part himself in giving effect to them. I will give here an outline of it, and some extracts—

[Carlingford here goes on to report in a slightly garbled form, the letter from Gladstone to Queen Victoria, dated Hawarden, 23 May 1885, which is printed virtually in full in *The Letters of Queen Victoria, Second Series*, iii, ed. G. E. Buckle, (London, 1928), pp. 652–5. Carlingford's inferior version is therefore omitted here. Gladstone's letter stated unequivocally that 'the proposal to re-enact the non-coercive provisions [of the Crimes Bill] for two years has, through reciprocal concessions, obtained the adhesion of the entire Cabinet.'

Gladstone went on to emphasize his desire to uproot the Dublin Castle system of centralized Irish government, and his fear of some future dishonourable surrender to Irish demands. Of the schemes proposed, that for a Central Board had 'been for

---

[1] A detailed account appeared in the *Birmingham Daily Post* on 22 May, greatly annoying Gladstone, who spoke of it at the Cabinet of 5 June.

many years desired' by him, and in matters of ordinary policy he would be willing to go farther than Chamberlain. Gladstone said that his view was 'undoubtedly that taken by the two markedly Radical ministers (as well as by others)'.

However, since Spencer and nearly all the Peer ministers favoured a system limited to County or Provincial government in Ireland, while Chamberlain and Dilke's group, including six of the eight Commons ministers, wished to base an elective Central Board on the County Boards, there was no point in taking the matter up in detail in Cabinet.]

Slept well. After luncheon walked up Craig Gowan, and sat —very low and hopeless. Read and copied Mr G's letter.[1] Dined with H.M. Sat between Princess Louise and Princess Beatrice.

Saturday 30 May. [At Balmoral.] Letter writing until luncheon— and in my room again until after 5, when I walked with Clinton[2] and Dr Reid[3] to Abergeldie. Met the Connaught children, the girl a spoilt little thing. Talk about the Queen's Household, etc. Management and economy improved by Cowell[4] but she gives him very little power. He gets on better since John Brown's disappearance from the scene.[5] *He* was all powerful—no servant

---

[1] Carlingford both talked with the Queen, and wrote her a letter, on the subject of Gladstone's communication. Carlingford's letter to the Queen (Royal Archives D/37/55) found in Gladstone's Irish plan 'no indication of an intention to bring it before the cabinet or to announce it to parliament' and surmised 'the letter looks like a political legacy.' The Queen wrote in her *Journal* (28 May): 'Talked to Lord Carlingford about Mr Gladstone's long letter on Irish measures, which Ld C thought a legacy. Parts he agreed with, but others, he would never be a party to.' In Oct. 1885 she showed the letter to Beach who sent it to Salisbury (Beach to Salisbury 14 Oct. 1885: Salisbury MSS.)

[2] Col. Lord Edward Pelham Clinton, K.C.B. (1836–1907), courtier, 2nd s. of fifth Duke of Newcastle: military career 1854–80; M.P. N. Notts. 1865–8; groom-in-waiting to the Queen, 1881–94; Master of the Household, 1894–1901.

[3] (Sir) James Reid (1849–1923), resident physician to Queen Victoria and Edward VII: entered the royal service in 1881 and succeeded Jenner in 1883; cr. Bt 1897; see Elizabeth Longford, 'Queen Victoria's Doctors', in Martin Gilbert, ed., *A Century of Conflict 1850–1950*, (London, 1966), pp. 75–87.

[4] Maj.-Gen. Sir John Clayton Cowell, K.C.B. (1832–94), soldier and courtier: governor to Prince Alfred 1856–65 and to Prince Leopold 1865–6; retired from army with rank of major-general, 1879; Master of H.M. Household 1866–94, when he died at Osborne.   [5] Brown d. 27 Mar. 1883.

had a chance of promotion except through him, and he favoured no man who didn't like his glass. Stories of his insolence. One day General Gardiner,[1] just come, shook hands with him, was very civil, and asked 'How is the Queen, and what is she saying?' Brown: 'Well she just said, Here's that damned fellow Gardiner come and he'll be poking his nose into everything!' One day John Brown was helplessly drunk at the Queen's door, and carried to bed. Dr Reid made H.M. very angry by telling her the real cause—she was sure it was strong tobacco. The Dr thinks she has not been the same to him since. Some of the courtiers were full of attentions to J.B., gave him presents etc—and he despised them for it. He was however unwearied and devoted in his attention to the Queen. Consumption of wine at Windsor—80 to 120 bottles a day.

Dined with the Queen . . . she was hot and unreasonable about the Russian negotiations.

Sunday 31 May. [After attending Crathie Church, near Balmoral, Carlingford talked a good deal with the preacher, Dr MacLeod.][2] . . . as to Disestablishment, the Church[3] had gained so much of late years, if she can hold her own for 10 years more she will be safe—the agitation much promoted by English Liberationists—most of the money comes from England. The Free Church has spoiled the Highlanders, made them fanatics, with their 'scowling Puritanism' . . .

Monday 1 June. [At Balmoral.] I have finished Ouida's *Puck*—unpleasant, exaggerated, overcoloured, extravagant, yet with a certain fascination. She knows the tremendous bodily charms that

---

[1] General (Sir) Henry Lynedoch Gardiner (1820–97), soldier and courtier: served in army 1837–67; groom-in-waiting, 1869–72, and equerry, 1872–96, to the Queen; K.C.V.O. 1897. A similar version of the anecdote concerning Gardiner may be found in Sir F. Ponsonby, *Recollections of Three Reigns* (London, 1951), p. 93, and is included in Tom Cullen, *The Empress Brown* (London, 1969), 183.

[2] '. . . Went to the Kirk at 12, where Dr Donald MacLeod, who arrived yesterday, performed the service, and preached a very fine sermon . . .' (*Queen Victoria's Journal*, 31 May.) MacLeod (1831–1916), the Queen's chaplain in Scotland, was successively minister in Lauderdale, Linlithgow, and Glasgow; Moderator of the Church of Scotland, 1894; not prominent in ecclesiastical politics.   [3] i.e. of Scotland.

woman has for man—and she knows that the good and evil of
the relations between man and woman cannot be truly judged
according to laws and conventionalities. When I read where
Ouida says that the *wife* is often not *the love* of a man's life, I turned
to my dead darling—my wife, my life, my own love, my passion,
my angel!

Wrote letters until luncheon. Consulted the Duchess of Rox-
burghe about a wedding present for Princess Beatrice—Nice
woman the Duchess. The Queen sent for me—long talk, in
Prince Albert's room, as usual. She wondered what Mr G. was
going to do—whether he would take a peerage etc. She talked
of the formation of his ministry, of the refusal of Granville and
Hartington, etc. I told her of Granville's letter to me at Montreux.[1]
She said she had been badly treated, that Mr G. had told her there
would be no *Radicals* in his Cabinet, that things were on that
footing for several days—then they were admitted.[2] Told her I
believed that when Mr. G. began to form a Cabinet, he did not
know that it would be necessary to admit Chamberlain and Dilke.
She is most afraid of Chamberlain, but she said his manner was
good. Dilke's not at all so—thought him very talkative and
'loud'—We talked of the Crimes Act—she said that the Prince of
Wales wrote that he would not hear of a 'Royal Residence', unless
there was a proper law to keep the peace, etc. She spoke of the
privately printed *Letters*[3] of her half sister, the Princess Hohenlohe,
to herself; of lines she had chosen from Poems by Dr Monsell[4] for
the seats to Prince Leopold,[5] and for something at Frogmore 'in
memory of my dear faithful friend'—i.e. John Brown. This
infatuation is wonderful. It is painfully absurd to hear his name

[1] In 1880 Granville had recalled a reluctant Carlingford from semi-retirement in
Switzerland, leading him to form hopes of high office which were frustrated till the
accident of Argyll's resignation in 1881.

[2] In fact only Chamberlain was admitted to the Cabinet in 1880, Dilke remaining outside as Under-Secretary for Foreign Affairs till 1882.

[3] On the death of Princess Feodora of Hohenlohe-Langenburg in 1872, Dean
Stanley prepared a strictly private edition of her letters to the Queen, as a family
keepsake. Stanley's work of 1873 forms the basis of the book by Harold A.
Albert, *Queen Victoria's Sister* (London, 1967).

[4] Dr J. S. B. Monsell (1811–75), a chaplain to the Queen and author of many
popular hymns and religious verses.   [5] Prince Leopold had died in 1884.

pronounced, when one would expect another. The Queen's political talk is very unsatisfactory—she has become a very bad politician, never showing any interest in or desire for reform or improvement. She was very kind—*told me to write to her*—sent me three books and two notes in the evening ... Dined with the Queen[1] ...

Tuesday 2 June. Left Balmoral early. To London by way of Edinburgh.

Wednesday 3 June. Most beautiful summer morning. At Hamilton Place [London] about 6. Went to bed for 3 or 4 hours ...

Thursday 4 June. Prepared a little for speaking. Drove to the Show ground at Waltham Abbey ... spoke very poorly—felt unfit for everything ... Escaped as soon as I could and drove home in the brougham.[2]

Friday 5 June. Dragged myself up to London for Cabinet at 11— most lovely day, and I longed to keep quiet. A cup of coffee at Athenaeum. Then to the Cabinet. The Budget came first. Childers proposed to reduce the increase on Spirit Duties from 2s. to 1s., and to increase the Wine Duty. Dilke made a statement against the latter, which was supported by Granville, on account of our difficult relations with France, and in the end by all the Cabinet including Mr. G, who supported Childers at first but afterwards advised him to leave Wine alone. Chamberlain pointed out that the rich were hit by the Income Tax and death duties, and that it was not necessary to tax them in another form as a set-off to the

---

[1] *Queen Victoria's Journal* contains no report of any conversation with Carlingford on 30 or 31 May or 1 June, though he dined with the Queen on each of those evenings.

[2] The occasion mentioned here was the annual Exhibition of the Essex Agricultural Society, at which Carlingford made a speech, frequently interrupted by applause, that exactly fitted the circumstances. He even boasted that, during his term of office, foot-and-mouth disease had become 'absolutely extinct' (*Essex County Standard*, 6 June 1885: cf. 25 June below, for similar remarks on foot-and-mouth).

Beer and Spirit Duties. Childers, however, said he could not consent, and left the room. Harcourt followed him, then Mr G., then Granville and the Chancellor were despatched. G. when he came back said it would be all right—that 'Childers had gone to consult a high authority on indirect taxation'—Mrs Childers no doubt. Childers has acted very weakly in all this Budget affair, and has lost himself in details. The decision against raising the Wine Duty was clearly right.[1] Then Mr G. made a statement—first about the 'leakage'[2] of the Cabinet which he said was a disgrace, and of bad augury for future governments. Then about the Crimes and Purchase Bills, and his mistake as to the consent of Chamberlain and Dilke to the latter.[3] Upon this Chamberlain stated the position of himself and Dilke (Lefevre taking same line). A Purchase Bill had been promised and could not now be withdrawn. He and Dilke were relieved of their compact. They would not now consent to any Crimes Bill unless it were either 1) passed for one year only, or 2) suspended, and not operative except by Order of the Queen in Council.—Some talk about the second alternative, which Chamberlain and Dilke have taken from Shaw Lefevre, and which Heneage has given notice of in the House of Commons.[4] *Harcourt said it was unconstitutional, and shocking to a Whig mind.* Chamberlain muttered that 'a Whig would swallow anything'—I mentioned great objections to it. Mr G. was favourable to it and sorry that he had an unfavourable letter from Spencer. Agreed that the question should be adjourned for Spencer to come.[5] Back to Dudbrook about 6—lovely evening.

[1] This decision was the main issue on which the Government was brought down on 8–9 June. Beach later also dropped the proposals to increase the taxes on beer and spirits, so that in the end there was no change in 1885 in the taxation of alcohol.

[2] An account of the Cabinet crisis appeared in the *Birmingham Daily Post* on 22 May.   [3] See entry of 21 May above.

[4] Heneage gave notice of his motion on 4 June. As well as pressing for only the most limited kind of special legislation for Ireland, it added that 'the present moment was favourable to the abolition of the present anomalous system of government in Ireland.' Heneage resigned office over Home Rule in the following spring.

[5] Gladstone, writing to the absent Spencer, told a different tale. In his account, the radicals' proposal to make the Crimes Act inoperative till brought into force by the executive, was supported by himself, Kimberley, Trevelyan, and Selborne: 'no one actually spoke in positive condemnation. Harcourt and Carlingford

Sunday 7 June. At Dudbrook. Gloomy day, without rain. Read in a desultory way. Talked to Constance.

Monday 8 June. Defeat on the Budget.[1]

To London early. Cabinet. Spencer had come for it. He stated his view of the question of the Crimes Bill (what Gladstone described in the House as 'the Bill to replace the Crimes Act'). He complained of having the question reopened after all the discussion it had received, and the concessions he had made. He was now called upon to allow the Bill to be inoperative until brought into force by Order in Council or Proclamation. He would consent to this, except as to the Intimidation or Boycotting clause—the Summary Jurisdiction—as to that he could not consent. Mr G. followed him at once, and gave his full support to that compromise, strongly advised the Cabinet to 'close with it'. He evidently hoped to carry Chamberlain and Dilke with him, but failed. Chamberlain would not hear of it—said it was no concession at all! etc. They have behaved very badly. Trevelyan refused to support Spencer! said he would have supported him if he had insisted on bringing the *other* parts of the Bill into immediate operation! Chamberlain has secured him and Lefevre. Agreement was evidently hopeless but the decision was adjourned.[2] Mr. G. said that Richard Grosvenor was not so confident as he had been about the division on the Budget, so, Mr G. said, this question may be settled in another way.

There was then some talk about the Zulfikar Pass. House of Lords. Seats Bill went through committee. A few changes of

---

appeared to attach great importance to one form of executive action rather than another. I think the leaning seemed to be in favour of proceeding by Proclamation' [rather than by Order in Council]. Gladstone ended by appealing to Spencer to agree to 'Lefevre's proposal': Spencer replied on 6 June 'At present I am clear I ought not to agree to it.' (B.M. Add. MS. 44312, ff. 128–30.)

[1] The division was in fact not taken till 1.45 a.m. on 9 June, ministers being defeated 264–252.

[2] Kimberley wrote '. . . nothing was finally settled when we resigned. Spencer would not give way nor would Chamberlain. The nearest approach to an agreement was on the plan of leaving it optional with the Lord Lieut. to bring the Act or any part of it into [action] by proclamation.' (Rosebery's notes on Kimberley's memoirs, Rosebery MSS.)

names—and a job about Jedburgh[1]—to take it out of the county of Roxburgh and so secure the latter for the Tories. Dined Brooks's. Talked to nobody.

Tuesday 9 June. At breakfast forgot at first the doubt about the Budget division—afterwards told Eddie[2] to look, who announced defeat of the Government by majority of 12—and a scene of great excitment in the House.

Cabinet at 12. Very unanimous and short. Mr G. said he should be glad to be able to make an announcement of the decision of the Cabinet as to the Crimes Bill, but he supposed he could not. This received in silence. Chamberlain and Dilke said nothing. He presumed he must at once tender resignation of Cabinet to the Queen. To this all agreed at once. Some talk as to order of proceedings in Parliament, and we broke up. A good deal said about the resignation of June 1868.[3] My darling, I thought of us two then and of myself now.

---

[1] Under the general agreement between the parties on redistribution, it was understood that Jedburgh, a solidly Liberal market town, and eight other towns which with it composed two burgh groups, should be merged with the surrounding county constituencies. Lord Lothian therefore sprang a surprise when on 8 June 1885 he made an unofficial proposal that Jedburgh alone should be treated exceptionally, by becoming part of the Border Burghs instead of the surrounding county of Roxburghshire. The amendment passed without debate (*Hansard*, vol. 298, cols. 1386–7), but was demolished by Trevelyan in the Commons as contravening vital principles as well as a private understanding (ibid., cols. 1572–6). When the amendment came up again in the Lords on 23 June, Lothian tried to divide, but three leaders of his own party at once intervened to prevent the matter going further (ibid., col. 1604). As the second largest Conservative landlord in the marginal constituency of Roxburghshire, Lothian was inevitably accused of trying 'to gerrymander the county for the purposes of the Tory party' (Arthur Elliot to Lothian, 23 June 1885: Lothian MSS., Scottish Record Office GD 40/16/32, ff. 3–5).

[2] Edward Strachey (1858–1936): M.P. (Lib.) S. Somerset 1892–1911; succ. father as Bt., 1891; Treasurer of H.M. Household 1905–10; cr. Baron Strachie, Nov. 1911; Paymaster-Genl. 1912–15; D.L., J.P., C.C. for Somerset; connected to Carlingford through his marriage to Constance, niece of Lady Waldegrave.

[3] The circumstances of 1868 came to mind because then, as in 1885, the introduction of a new franchise which could not become operative until the autumn meant that there could be no question of a dissolution following a parliamentary defeat. For the contretemps over this issue in 1868 (actually in Apr.–May, not June) see R. Blake, *Disraeli* (London, 1966), pp. 500–3.

To the Levée—Derby said there was one exception to the happy faces round the Cabinet table—the Prime Minister—Granville had made this remark. The Parnellites were indecent in their triumph at the division—some called 'Buckshot'—somebody 'Foxy Jack' (Spencer)—somebody 'Myles Joyce'[1]! . . .

Wednesday 10 June. To Weald[2] before luncheon. . . . Opened the bazaar by making a little speech to a very small audience—Bazaar for Drill Hall[3] . . .

Thursday 11 June. Beautiful day . . . Back to London after breakfast. Office. Went to Grosvenor Gallery. Millais' portrait of Gladstone for Ch.Ch. hall very fine. Dined at home.

Friday 12 June. Office at 12. Glasgow deputation about Foreign Animals Wharf.[4] House of Lords committee. Considered the Poor Law Guardians Bill—only three voted against the Conservative majority, Monk Bretton, Powerscourt, and myself. Powerscourt[5] very happy at getting an English peerage!

Salisbury went to Balmoral last night.[6] Kimberley read the Seats Bill a 3rd time by consent. Salisbury wrote to him—'I am starting for Balmoral. This is being *sent for* with a vengeance' . . .

Northbrook came—arranged to give him up the house[7] on Monday week . . .

[1] Joyce was one of three men hanged in connection with the Maamtrasna murders of 1882, the conviction in his case being allegedly discredited by subsequent confessions.

[2] Weald Hall, Brentwood, Essex, home of C. J. H. Tower (1841–1924), a Tory country gentleman who was an Essex J.P., D.L., and high sheriff.

[3] The fête raised £400 to build a drill hall for the Essex Volunteers. Carlingford's introductory speech again showed his easy touch in performing his social duties as Lord-Lieutenant (*Essex Weekly News*, 12 June).

[4] The deputation requested permission, which the Privy Council eventually granted, to put up new buildings at Govan for the landing of Canadian cattle (*Glasgow Herald*, 13 June 1885).

[5] An Irish representative peer, created baron in the peerage of the United Kingdom, 27 June 1885: offered junior office by Gladstone, Feb. 1886.

[6] Salisbury left Arlington St. at 7.45 p.m. on 11 June to catch the night train for Scotland. (Cranborne to Churchill n.d. [11 June 1885], Churchill MSS. v. 1264.)

[7] Hamilton Place, London, a house belonging to Northbrook but placed at Carlingford's disposal while in office.

Saturday 13 June. [At Dudbrook.] I have come down here this evening. . . . Mundella came and sat some time. He talked of Gladstone with no liking—of his neglect of any personal attention to or recognition of his friends etc. We talked of the wretched Egyptian policy or want of policy of the Govt. In going out of office—he is well satisfied, *because he gets rid of the transfer of Scotch Education to the Scotch Secretary*, because he has brought in the Welsh Intermediate Education Bill,[1] and for other reasons. We are good friends[2]—but he is a difficult and most encroaching Vice-President for a President of the Council to act with.

. . . Here about 6.30. Saw first hay cut. Read *Romola* in the clematis arbour—it is over elaborate and painfully reflective . . . My soul sinks within me from desolation and hopelessness—my love my love how am I to live?

Sunday 14 June. Today I have too much given myself up to 'chance desires'. Sat in the little library and the arbour, reading more or less of many books,—the Fortescue History, French plays, *Romola*, Mill's *Logic*, and the *Nouvelle Héloise*—I can answer for the truth of the descriptions of passion in that book—. . .

Monday 15 June. Back to London . . . Office. House of Lords. The adjournment to Friday [19 June] was moved by Cranbrook,[3] to the disgust of the Duke of Richmond.[4] On my way to Hill St. I met Dodson (Monk Bretton) riding, who told me of a

---

[1] This important bill was withdrawn by the Conservatives on 9 July 1885 without a debate or division having taken place upon it, legislation on the subject eventually being passed in 1887.

[2] Curiously, Mundella was probably the only colleague to whom Carlingford offered hospitality in 1885. A letter from Carlingford of 28 July 1885 (Mundella MSS., f. ii) contains arrangements for Mundella to visit Dudbrook, though it is reasonably clear that this fell through for some reason.

[3] Gathorne Hardy, 1st Earl of Cranbrook (1814–1906): M.P. (Cons.) Leominster 1856–65 and Oxford University 1865–78 where he defeated Gladstone; a protégé of Disraeli who made him Home Sec. 1867–8, Sec. for war 1874–8, and Indian Sec. 1879–80; Lord President 1885–6 and 1886–92; cr. Viscount 1878 and Earl 1892; unexpectedly recovered from a severe illness, spring 1885.

[4] 6th Duke of Richmond and Lennox, and 1st Duke of Gordon (1818–1903): M.P. (Cons.) W. Sussex 1841–60; President of Poor Law Board 1859, and of Board of Trade 1867–8; Lord President of the Council 1874–80, June–Aug. 1885;

strange scene in the House of Commons—Randolph Churchill had opposed the change put into the Seats Bill by Kimberley at the desire of Salisbury, for hastening the date when the new franchise should take effect, and Parliament could be dissolved. Upon this he divided against Sir Stafford Northcote, and had Hicks Beach[1] with him. After the division Randoph Churchill said in a loud whisper to the Treasury bench 'This puts you fellows back again'. Gorst said to Mundella 'We are determined not to have the *old gang*.'[2]

Tuesday 16 June. A meeting at Mr G's—not in the Cabinet Room. Granville, Hartington, Rosebery, Trevelyan absent. Gladstone had summoned us on account of a visit he had had from Arthur Balfour, who came from Salisbury to ask whether Mr G. would give certain assurances—namely that he and his colleagues would not oppose the new Govt taking the time of the House, when they wanted it for Supply—and 2) that if the House did not accept their financial proposals, would not oppose their obtaining the necessary money by borrowing—by Exchequer bills. Mr G. had been very cautious in his answer—wished to have it in writing— must consult his colleagues—such application should be made through the Queen. W. Harcourt, Chamberlain, Dilke, and Mr G. himself strongly against the 2nd promise, and [word illegible] less strongly against the 1st.

At the end of the discussion Gladstone wrote memorandum of an answer to be given to A. Balfour. Kimberley had a note from Salisbury about the Commons Amendments to the Re-distribution Bill, saying that 'a very serious constitutional difficulty had arisen.' Harcourt walked with R. Churchill who was so discreet that Harcourt concluded he had been 'squared'.

---

first holder of new Scottish office Aug. 1885–Jan. 1886, despite his view that the new department was superfluous; declined office July 1886 and went into retirement.

[1] Sir Michael Edward Hicks Beach Bt. (1837–1916), Churchill's closest colleague 1885–6: M.P. Gloucestershire 1864–5, W. Bristol 1885–1906; junior office 1868; Chief Sec. for Ireland 1874–8, 1886–7, resigning on grounds of ill health; Colonial Sec. 1878–80, Chancellor of the Exchequer 1885–6, 1895–1902; cr. Viscount 1906 and Earl 1916.

[2] This move by the 'Fourth Party' was defeated by 333 to 35.

Read at Athenaeum. Dined at home. Constance[1] and Eddie excited about the crisis. Went to Hill St.[2]

Wednesday 17 June. Gladstone has declined an Earldom.[3]

A yellow Box came from Mr G. this morning with a memorandum explaining what he meant to do. He will take his seat on the front Opposition bench, but will absent himself for a time for the sake of his voice. He will be only physically not morally absent. This will be his position till the end of the session. He cannot perceive or confidently anticipate any state of facts *which would change his long cherished desire and purpose to withdraw at the end of the present Parliament from active participation in politics.*

At work until luncheon going through papers, destroying etc.

Read my letters from Granville and Gladstone when this Govt was formed in '80 . . .

. . . Council Office—Disagreeable interview with Craik,[4] clever, disagreeable, intriguing man, about an article written by him in the *Fortnightly* in favour of a 'Minister of Education', published without my permission or knowledge. He said he had obtained the permission of the Vice-President[5]—a bad incident of the 'Dual Control'—I have left a minute disapproving of this as a breach of discipline . . .

Thursday 18 June. To Board at South Kensington.—Saw Col. Murdoch Smith,[6] whom I have appointed Director of the Edinburgh Museum, just from Teheran, said that the Russian

---

[1] Only child of the noted tenor Charles B. Braham, and hence niece of Lady Waldegrave: m. Edward Strachey (see note 2 on p. 113 above); d. 1936.

[2] To visit his brother Lord Clermont who had come to London to consult specialists at the onset of what proved to be a fatal illness.

[3] The honour was offered by the Queen on 13 June and declined by Gladstone the following day (J. Morley, *The Life of William Ewart Gladstone*, iii (London, 1903), 209).

[4] Henry Craik (1846–1927), civil servant in the education department from 1870: sec., Scottish Education Dept., 1885–1904; his 'faults of personality' noted by a subsequent Scottish Sec. (Lothian to Salisbury, 15 Aug. 1892: Salisbury MSS.) He was later M.P. (Cons.) for a Scottish University seat 1906–27 showing strong reactionary sentiments.   [5] Mundella.

[6] Col. Robert Murdoch Smith (1835–1900): soldier (1855–60); explorer and archaeologist at his own expense in Cyrenaica 1860–2; director of Persian section

reinforcements which had crossed the Caspian did not exceed 5,000 men, and that the whole force east of the Caspian was about 15,000. . . . Bid goodbye to Donnelly,[1] Armstrong,[2] etc, believing this to be my last official day there—Will it be so?

Summoned to Downing St. at 12.30—we met in the Cabinet Room. Granville and Hartington again absent, at Ascot. Rosebery came from there late. I said—Does this mean that we are to begin again? Lord Selborne treated that as impossible. Mr G. stated that he had received Lord Salisbury's application through A. Balfour in writing (Arthur Balfour's), had answered as arranged on Tuesday, and now had received from the Queen a letter from Lord Salisbury to her repeating the application, with the Queen's hope that it would be acceded to. He read and showed us Salisbury's letter, and his own answer to the Queen. Salisbury based his application for assurances upon the *impossibility of dissolving*. This was discussed and the Law Officers sent for, who arrived as the Cabinet broke up. It appears that there will be no legal power of dissolution, as soon as the Redistribution Bill becomes law. Mr G. was going to the Queen, to be there at 3. His language to her was agreed upon—no specific pledges, but general assurances to be liberally given . . .

Friday 19 June. . . . Slaved at sorting and destroying papers, etc. Luncheon Brooks's.

To House of Lords. Salisbury moved to postpone the consideration of the Seats Bill (Commons Amendments) until Tuesday. Kimberley resisted, and we divided.[3] Kimberley told me

of Anglo-Indian telegraph 1865–85; app. director of Science and Art Museum, Edinburgh, 2 May 1885; Kt. 1888. See W. K. Dickson, *The Life of Major-General Sir Robert Murdoch Smith* (Edinburgh and London, 1901).

[1] Col. J. F. D. Donnelly (1834–1902) was Secretary of the Science and Art Dept. which was responsible for South Kensington, and secretary to the informal committee which actually administered it; C.B. 1886; K.C.B. 1893.

[2] Thomas Armstrong (1832–1911): professional artist, and friend of Whistler; director of the art division of the Science and Art Dept., 1881–98.

[3] For a full account of this argument between Salisbury and Kimberley see *Hansard*, vol. 298, col. 1592. After complaining that the Redistribution Bill prevented an election before November, Salisbury carried his motion of adjournment by 124 to 56.

things were in an 'acute stage'—Gladstone beginning to think of coming in again. Mr G., in a box, reported his interviews with the Queen yesterday—she very gracious—begged him to put down for her the principal points, which he did—While there telegram came from Salisbury saying that 'in the unanimous opinion of those who would form his Cabinet, Mr G's declaration was of no value.' Extraordinary state of things—the Salisbury Cabinet named—Sir Stafford Northcote deposed from the leadership in favour of Hicks Beach—Sir Stafford to go to the House of Lords as *Earl* of Iddesleigh—and take First Lord of the Treasury, but not Prime Minister.

Constance and I dined together. A great deal of talk.

Saturday 20 June. Chamberlain made a speech[1] on Thursday which might have been made by Parnell or Healy.

Cabinet at 11. All there except Hartington and Rosebery.[2] It was to consider another letter from Salisbury to the Queen. This took no notice of Mr G's general assurances and repeated the specific pledges he required. A good deal of discussion, but no one thought that the pledges could be given, and an answer by Mr G. was agreed to, which included regret that the assurance given was not accepted. (Mr G. had written for the Queen on Thursday, to be given to Lord Salisbury, the following—'in my opinion the real value of such a declaration lies in the spirit in which it is given and taken—I can say for myself and friends that we should interpret and act upon mine in the spirit in which the Seats Bill arrangement was made and observed.' This was the substance.) It seemed to me that Mr G. and most of the Cabinet

[1] Delivered on Wed. 17 June at Holloway Hall, West Islington, and reported in *The Times*, 18 June, p. 7. After a prolonged attack on Conservative opportunism, he turned his attention to the conduct of the Liberal ministry in Ireland, denouncing them for relying 'on the bayonets of 30,000 soldiers encamped permanently as in a hostile country . . . the time has come to reform altogether the absurd and irritating anachronism which is known as Dublin Castle, to sweep away altogether these alien boards of foreign officials, and to substitute for them a genuine administration of purely Irish business.' Ten days later *United Ireland*, representing Nationalist policy, began a campaign of abuse against Chamberlain.

[2] Spencer, being in Ireland, was also absent, and was not summoned to London till Sunday 21 June.

wished to return to office. Trevelyan spoke of our having much less difficulty among ourselves about Irish affairs. Lord Selborne questioned this and so did I. W. Harcourt agreed with Trevelyan. Dilke thought that Salisbury would go on, even if the assurances were refused—a talk with A. Balfour had seemed to show this. Spencer has postponed his departure. Northbrook and I have stopped our preparations . . .

Sunday 21 June. . . . Restless and harassed and miserable. Henry Grenfell to breakfast. A great deal of talk, much about Gladstone—said I disliked him more than ever. Childers says the same according to Henry Grenfell. For luncheon to Lady Molesworth . . .

. . . Emly said it was generally understood that Lord Salisbury would give up. Found that there had been a Cabinet summoned. Went to Kimberley (after trying Childers and Trevelyan.) Kimberley told me all about it. It was on account of an appeal from the Queen, to which Mr G. gave a civil answer, but no more! only Lord Selborne, Kimberley, Chamberlain, and Dilke were there—and Henry James came—He has now discovered that the Reform Acts of '32 and of '67 contained words saving the right of the Crown *to dissolve*—At those times a demise of the Crown dissolved the Parliament. Something important may possibly come out of this fact. Mr G. is evidently preparing to come back. He and also Kimberley *wrote to Spencer pressing him to come over at once, as everything would turn on the Irish question.*[1] H. James had heard of language used by Northcote which implied a dissolution under the existing law.

Despatch received from Col. Ridgway[2] (on the Afghan bound-

[1] Gladstone wrote '. . . undoubtedly your presence here is absolutely indispensable in a certain contingency, namely that of our retaining or resuming office, for the gravest matter . . . we should then have to consider would be that connected with the Crimes Act . . .' Despite the Queen's effort to induce Salisbury to take office, Gladstone could not 'say that the odds lie on that side' (Gladstone to Spencer, 21 June 1885; Spencer MSS., in packet marked Trevelyan). Cf. 'I should say the betting is 3 to 2 that Mr Gladstone has to return . . .' (E. Hamilton to Spencer, 21 June 1885: Spencer MSS.)

[2] Col. Joseph West Ridgeway (1844–1930): served in Afghan war 1879–80; Under-Sec. to Govt. of India 1880–5; member of commission appointed in Apr. 1885 to negotiate the Russo-Afghan boundary; Under-Sec. at Dublin Castle 1887–93; K.C.S.I. 1885.

ary). He says that if the Russians had delayed their attack on Penjdeh for a week, the Tekke's would have risen against them. Great difficulties about transport and supplies. Without Persia movement of large bodies of troops impossible.

Monday 22 June. Visits from Arran[1] and Sir Thos. May.[2] May thought that Salisbury would give up, but agreed with me that he ought to go on, and that his requirements of specific pledges from Mr G. were unreasonable, as well as unnecessary.

. . . To the office. C. Peel knew nothing. He had told the Duke of Richmond what I said about our promises and intentions. To Athenaeum. Talked to Aberdare,[3] and to Huxley,[4] who was very cordial—I have been fighting for his pension.

. . . H. Leeson[5] had heard from Lowther[6] and others at the Turf that Salisbury had undertaken the Govt. E. Hamilton, H. Calcraft,[7] and H. James were dining together close to me—Hamilton said that this news was 'quite premature' but James told me he

---

[1] 5th Earl of Arran, K.P. (1839–1901): owned 30,000 acres in Mayo of annual value £7000; cr. a baron in the U.K. peerage, 1884, but generally regarded as outside politics.

[2] Sir Thomas Erskine May (1815–86): clerk of the House of Commons 1871–86; cr. Baron Farnborough 1886.

[3] H. A. Bruce, first Baron Aberdare (1815–95): Home Sec. 1868–73; cr. peer 1873; Lord President 1873–4; in later life prominent in Welsh affairs, especially education.

[4] Thomas Henry Huxley (1825–95), scientist and polemicist: chief inspector of salmon fisheries 1881–May 1885; Dean and Professor of biology in the Normal School of Science, South Kensington 1881–5; granted two pensions, one on the civil list, of £1500 p.a. total value, Dec. 1885, having given up nearly all his appointments on doctor's orders.

[5] Hon. Henry Leeson (1837–91), 3rd s. of 5th Earl of Milltown: chamberlain to L.L. of Ireland, 1859–66, 1869–74; succ. as 7th and last Earl, 1890.

[6] James Lowther (1840–1904), former Conservative minister: M.P., with short breaks, 1865–1904; held junior office, 1868, 1874–8; Chief Sec. for Ireland, 1878–80; a protectionist; curiously passed over by Salisbury in 1885 and 1886.

[7] Henry George Calcraft (1836–96), civil servant: clerk, Board of Trade, 1852, and private sec. to its president 1859–74 (including Carlingford's term of office there); asst. sec. to its railway dept. 1874–86, and perm. sec. to the Board of Trade 1886–93, retiring on a pension of £1,200; pilloried by Disraeli in *Lothair* as Mr Pinto, but compiled *The Wit and Wisdom of Lord Beaconsfield* (1881); K.C.B., 1890; described as 'that repository of all gossip' (Harcourt to Chamberlain, 23 Nov. 1885; Chamberlain MSS. JC 5/38/37).

had very little doubt of its truth. This is a relief to me—I have
been sick with doubt and nervousness all day.

Tuesday 23 June. The papers made an almost positive announcement of Salisbury's acceptance—a great relief to me in spite of
the great changes it will make in my life, the hopelessness of that
life itself, and my dependence upon Clermont. Northbrook came.
Told him what a great comfort and advantage his house had been
to me during my four years of office. The arrangement suited him
but for me it was of the greatest importance. Arranged with Fitch
for moving, and worked at books and papers. To the office.
Cranbrook succeeds me—the Duke of Richmond taking the Board
of Trade for the convenience of his friends—Stanhope[1] succeeds
Mundella with a seat in the Cabinet— . . .

. . . Saw Dasent, come from Dublin with his chief[2] for nothing.
Spencer was in the House of Lords, but with his usual want of
cordiality did not come near me. From what Dasent told me,
Spencer would not have gone on without a Crimes Bill, and
would not have yielded to the plea of *non possumus.*—Dasent said
he believes Hartington would have gone with him. The
Chancellor, Northbrook, and I would have done the same.

Wednesday 24 June. Out of office.
. . . To Windsor to resign.—In the saloon carriage were the
Prince of Wales, Gladstone, Lord Selborne, Harcourt, Hartington,
Derby, Granville, Kimberley, Trevelyan, Childers—Talked to the
Prince of Wales (which I have not done for a long time) and to Mr
G. He told me all about negotiations of Sunday and Monday.[3]

[1] Hon. Edward Stanhope (1840–93), second son of the 5th Earl Stanhope: M.P.
(Cons.) Lincolnshire 1874–93; junior office 1875–80; played a leading part in
Conservative party organization 1878–85; Vice-President of the Council June–
Aug. 1885 with seat in Cabinet; President of Board of Trade Aug. 1885–Jan. 1886;
Colonial Sec. 1886–7; War Sec. 1887–92.

[2] Spencer.

[3] This was the only occasion on which Gladstone spoke agreeably to Carlingford in 1885. Gladstone's unwonted display of amenity must be considered in the
light of his conversation of 18 June with Rosebery, when they agreed that
Carlingford should be dropped if the Liberals returned to office (R. R. James,
Rosebery, p. 170).

The question was not absolutely decided by Salisbury until Tuesday morning. . . . W. Harcourt's opinion is that the Queen has greatly weakened the Tories, *stimulated the democratic movement*, and assisted the Liberal party by encouraging Lord Salisbury to take office. We should have broken up, he said (having said the contrary at the last Cabinet[1]), but Gladstone was determined to form a Govt again, upon Salisbury refusing, no matter how many left him. Harcourt says G. will form a Govt after the General Election! *Granville told me that Harcourt had put himself entirely at Gladstone's disposal.*—Harcourt told me that he had told Mr G. he could form a Govt with 'any dozen men he liked—it didn't matter who they were—as strong a Govt. as the present, probably stronger'! He must think this flattery to be his best game.

. . . Saw the Queen before the Council—she very cordial and most kind—said she would not ask me to the wedding—thought that weddings did not suit me etc.—after a good deal of talk she got up, and gave me her hand, which I kissed warmly and sincerely.[2]

. . . The other ministers had short audiences, particularly W. Harcourt, and we got away. Hartington talked in the train— thought Mr G. very ill pleased at the result . . .

Thursday 25 June. Did not go again to the office, so I have probably left it for ever. C. Peel at Windsor was very warm in his regrets at the change, so far as I am concerned—He and I have been upon the friendliest and pleasantest terms. I have made no reputation but I have done well at the Council Office. The undefined and awkward relations between the President of the Council and the

[1] Harcourt in fact gave this opinion at the penultimate meeting on Saturday 20 June.

[2] 'Lord Carlingford was much affected when I spoke to him, saying I had been so kind to him, and still more so when I took leave': extract from the Queen's journal, 24 June 1885, in *The Letters of Queen Victoria 1862–85*, iii (ed. G. E. Buckle), 679. It was probably on this occasion that Carlingford told the Queen 'it would have been impossible to serve again with Chamberlain after his speeches on leaving office' (Cranbrook's diary, 14 Aug. 1885, reporting conversation with the Queen on 11 Aug. 1885).

Vice-President, and now the Chancellor of the Duchy,[1] are a great drawback. Chaplin[2] succeeds Trevelyan.[3] I have not left a single case of Foot and Mouth behind me . . .

Tuesday 30 June. . . . Rosebery made a speech[4] on Monday [29 June] at Edinburgh at which a letter was read from Mr Gladstone which seems to mean that he has changed his mind and will stand again for Midlothian as leader of the Liberal Party. Rosebery goes in evidently for Chamberlain's national Council in Dublin.[5]

Saturday 4 July. . . . McMurtrie sends me a heavy list of arrears.[6] He hears that Lord Pembroke[7] in Wiltshire has arrears mounting to £80,000. I have just borrowed £2,000 from Scotts[8] on a promissory note to pay estate charges and carry on the sinking at Radstock. They have just cut another seam of coal.

[1] This rather conflicts with Carlingford's evidence to Childers' committee on educational administration, when he painted a rosy picture of concord and harmony (*Parl. Papers*, 1884, XIII, pp. 34–43). The reference to the Chancellor of the Duchy of Lancaster arises from a decision made in 1883 to create an agricultural department of the Privy Council under a committee of four or five ministers. The spokesman for this committee in the House of Commons, and its chairman when the Lord President of the Council was absent, was to be the Chancellor of the Duchy of Lancaster. This lightened Carlingford's responsibilities as regards daily administration without creating a minister with undivided responsibility for agriculture.

[2] Henry Chaplin (1841–1923): M.P. Lincolnshire seats 1868–1906, Surrey 1907–16; Cabinet minister 1889–92, 1895–1900; bankrupt landowner and Protectionist; in close touch with Churchill 1885 and critical of the existing leadership; cr. Viscount, 1916.

[3] As Chancellor of the Duchy of Lancaster outside the Cabinet, with responsibility for agriculture.

[4] See *The Times*, 30 June 1885, p. 6.

[5] Cf. Rosebery to Chamberlain, 20 May 1885 (Chamberlain MSS. JC 5/65/1), saying 'my practical knowledge of Ireland is almost nil' but approving 'some such scheme as yours'.

[6] Cf. McMurtrie to Carlingford, 2 July 1885, Waldegrave MSS: 'As regards the colliery . . . in thirty years' experience I have never before known money so difficult.'

[7] 13th Earl of Pembroke (1850–95), a relatively minor figure in politics who had nevertheless formed hopes of becoming leader of the Conservative party at the time of the Reform crisis in autumn 1884.

[8] Scott and Co., bankers, 1 Cavendish Sq., London.

Monday 6 July. Parliament met again and there were statements by Salisbury and Carnarvon,[1] answered by Kimberley, Granville being in the gout—but I did not go up.

Wednesday 8 July. . . . *There is to be no Crimes Bill,* and the decision is justified by Carnarvon, Hicks Beach and R. Churchill[2] on the ground not of impossibility *but of principle*! They may possibly succeed—they are far more likely to do so than *we* should have been—but Davitt[3] is preaching No Rent. It's a strange state of things and casts a cloud over Spencer's retirement. That question really ended Gladstone's Govt. If we had been agreed upon that, I can't doubt that the Budget defeat would have been prevented or got over.

Friday 10 July. To London with difficulty—day so lovely . . . The Duke of Argyll made his speech[4] upon the change of Govt—entirely an attack upon his friends?—the late Govt. He fell foul of Chamberlain with justice, and of Rosebery[5] for his speech at Edinburgh. He ended by the exclamation, 'Happy is the land that hath its quiver full of'—Argylls!—of 'men not sheep'. He might have made an effective protest against the cry of 'the Grand Old Man', as the bond of Liberal unity, and against the swallowing of Chamberlain's Irish policy—('restoration of the Heptarchy', he

[1] 4th Earl of Carnarvon (1831–90): Colonial Sec. 1866–7 (resigning over Disraeli's Reform Bill), and 1874–8 (resigning over the Eastern Question); the Conservatives' controversial L.L. of Ireland 1885–6; dropped from the party leadership, July 1886. For Carnarvon's statement on 6 July in which he announced that the Conservatives would not renew the Crimes Act, see *Hansard*, vol. 298, cols. 1652–62.

[2] Statements by Beach on 7 July (*Hansard*, vol. 298, col. 1839), and by Churchill, 8 July (ibid., col. 1866).

[3] Michael Davitt (1846–1906), militant Irish Nationalist and land reformer: imprisoned 1870–7 and 1881–2; formed Land League, 1877, and the National League, 1882; before 1890 a radical critic of the Nationalist leadership, thereafter a pillar of the anti-Parnellites; M.P. 1892–1900; see F. Sheehy-Skeffington, *Michael Davitt*, ed. F.S.L. Lyons (London, 1967).

[4] *Hansard*, vol. 299, col. 246, 10 July 1885.

[5] Cf. Rosebery's journal, 10 July: 'The D. of Argyll made a long omnium gatherum speech in which he dealt so much with my Edinburgh speech that I had to get up after him and having nothing to say spoke quite inconceivably ill'.

said), but the speech was wanting, as so often the case with him, in sound sense and grasp of the subject and situation, and full of the assumption of superior wisdom, and morality. . . . Walked up with Northbrook. . . . We talked of the future. He said, 'Gladstone and I agree about very few things', and 'neither of us is likely to be in Gladstone's next Cabinet'.

Monday 13 July. Hill St. . . . Surprised at the number of letters from Gladstone in '69 and '70—about the Irish Bills principally— my work was more important at that time than it has ever been since. . . . Dined with the Mays—to meet the Gladstones—no talk with him. Took Mrs Gladstone to dinner. She asked me how I understood Mr G's Midlothian letter—said I didn't understand it. She implied that he had not decided whether to go on or not[1]—'*he would not unless he saw a great work to be done.*'

Friday 17 July. . . . Today in the Lords there have been three subjects in which I might naturally have taken part[2]—it was a question of imperfect obligation whether I should go up for them, but it would have been the energetic thing to do—and I could not bring myself to do it. . . . *I am broken down in mind and nerve*—How am I to live? I can't long bear this place [Dudbrook, Essex]—though I love it.

---

[1] Gladstone left his wife very uncertain about his intentions. 'As to his own inclination for retirement it was, if it is not now, as clear as the day!' Mrs Gladstone wrote (to Lady Lucy Cavendish, 4 July: Hawarden MSS.), ascribing his change of heart to last minute pressure from Granville and Harcourt. Of Gladstone's letter to his Midlothian constituents, his wife wrote 'It is curious the different ways of taking it. I must own that I could hardly see any other meaning than the one that he is most likely to stand again!' (Hawarden MSS., n.d.). Gladstone had an obvious tactical use for his threats of retirement, as a means of bringing a disunited front bench to heel, but he went far beyond that in creating a belief in those closest to him that he would not be leader at the next election. Rosebery, for instance, had fixed up a candidate to fight Midlothian in lieu of Gladstone (T. G. Carmichael to Rosebery, 11 Apr., 15 May 1885, Rosebery MSS., box 61). As late as 10 July 1885 it was possible for Gladstone to talk of feeling that if he was to be returned for Midlothian, it must be as a private member, the only alternative being his not standing at all (Rosebery's journal, 10 July 1885).

[2] On 17 July the Lords debated secondary education, imperial defence and Ashbourne's land purchase bill.

Saturday 18 July. To London by 8.37 train. . . . The treatment of Parnell's motion[1] (for fresh inquiry into the Maamtrasna and other trials) and of Spencer by Hicks Beach, R. Churchill, and Gorst[2] evidently very bad.

. . . George Hamilton came to Goschen after the debate to talk about the Committee on Admiralty Finance, of which Goschen is chairman, and he said he was so sickened by what had just been going on that he couldn't speak to him.

Sunday 19 July. . . . Read the Land Purchase (Ireland) Bill.[3] I greatly distrust the effects—perhaps not immediate—of the immense temptation the State will hold out to the tenants to buy their holdings, the pressure that may be brought to bear upon landlords to sell, and the increased difficulty of maintaining rent.

Monday 20 July. . . . House of Lords . . . Spencer was waiting to make a speech on the 2nd Reading of Land Purchase (Ireland) Bill, and saying how he hated it, but it grew late and he put it off.

Tuesday 21 July. . . . House of Lords—Spencer criticized the Purchase Bill.[4]

[1] *Hansard*, vol. 299, col. 1064, 17 July 1885. Parnell was overheard saying excitedly to Healy during the debate 'This is the greatest thing we have ever accomplished' (Rosebery's journal, 3 Sept. 1885). The public appearance of Conservative compliance with Irish demands was engineered by a 'Fourth Party' plot, entirely unsanctioned by the Cabinet, and in defiance of Salisbury and Carnarvon who had strongly opposed reopening the Maamtrasna case (Carnarvon to Beach, 15 July 1885: St. Aldwyn MSS. PCC/78: Salisbury to Beach, 16 July PCC/69).

[2] Sir John Gorst (1835–1911): Solicitor-General and an intimate of Churchill in the Fourth Party.

[3] 48 & 49 Vict., c. 73: known as 'Lord Ashbourne's Act'.

[4] *Hansard*, vol. 299, col. 1342, 21 July 1885. Carlingford also spoke, in what was to be his last speech in parliament, though he lived till 1898. He made a confident and powerful general defence of the 1881 Land Act against a gratuitous attack by Argyll, at the same time remarking of Ashbourne's bill 'I wish it all possible success', giving vent to the misgivings recorded above only in muted form.

... Dined Brooks's—Talked to Tweeddale.[1] Said he and other landlords in his part of Scotland were in a very bad way.—A £1,000 a year farm near him just out of lease—highest rent offered for it, not by the old tenant, £600. These farms are largely reclaimed from the moor.

... Gibson, Lord Ashbourne,[2] struck one as a new phenomenon in the House of Lords—too loud for 'the class of Vere de Vere' but promises to be popular.

Thursday 23 July. ... Until luncheon—destroyed and arranged papers from Hamilton Place—accumulations of these four years— many about the Land Act and its working.

Friday 24 July. ... Dined at the dinner to Spencer for which I had come up—at Westminster Palace Hotel—nearly 200 dined. I was very badly placed—probably Heneage's[3] doing. Sat between Kensington and Mundella. Monson[4] said W. Harcourt seemed to have gone off his head—he had abused Granville to him in an outrageous way. He stopped me in Pall Mall today, and did the same.

Only four speeches and 3 speakers at the dinner, Hartington, Spencer, Bright, but Hartington and Spencer were an hour each—

[1] 10th Marquess (1826–1911): Lib. M.P. 1865–8 and 1878; owned 43,000 acres, value £26,000 p.a., in W. Lothian and Berwick; Unionist, 1886; a conscientious resident landlord, thought by county society to be very radical in his views.

[2] Edward Gibson (1837–1913), cr. Baron Ashbourne, 1885: Lord Chancellor of Ireland, with seat in the Cabinet, 1885–6, 1886–92, 1895–1905; a member of the 'Shadow Cabinet' under both Disraeli and Bonar Law; described by the Queen as 'a clever, agreeable man, with a strong Irish accent, and saying everything that comes into his head' (*Queen Victoria's Journal*, 15 Aug. 1885); on the basis of his parliamentary virtuosity in opposition, 1880–5, was regarded in June 1885 as a past master of Irish politics, but his floundering and volatility when in office had left him all but discredited by Jan. 1886; because of supposed connivance with Nationalists, was 'cut by the Dublin Loyalists ... No one will talk to him at the Kildare St Club—everyone refuses to play whist with him. He is regularly boycotted ...' (Albert Grey to 3rd Earl Grey, 15 Jan. 1886, Grey MSS.)

[3] Edward Heneage (1840–1922), M.P. (Lib.) Grimsby since 1880: Lincolnshire landowner; Chancellor of the Duchy of Lancaster, Feb.–Apr. 1886; resigned Apr. 1886 over Home Rule; chairman of the Liberal Unionist Party 1893–8.

[4] 7th Baron Monson (1829–1898): captain of the Yeomen of the Guard 1880–5, 1886; first and only Viscount Oxenbridge, cr. 1886.

too long, and not very good. Old Bright spoke of the Parnellites with great severity.

At Spencer's dinner met Errington[1]—now Sir George Errington, Bart. Said he had been told by Armstrong that they greatly regretted me at South Kensington. Armstrong said I 'was a model Lord President'.

This same Friday Chamberlain made a very clever speech at Hackney,[2] and spoke well as to Spencer[3] and the Tories. I met him the other day at Brooks's—he said 'Are you shocked to see me in these sacred precincts?' He was looking for H. James. He is decidely agreeable in private life. He talked of the dealings between Randolph Churchill and the Parnellites[4]—said the latter *now* repudiated his plan of 'local Govt' which they had before

---

[1] George Errington (1839–1920): Irish M.P. (Lib.) 1874–85; unofficial British agent at the Vatican 1881–5; accepted baronetcy on Gladstone's recommendation, June 1885; while occupied in Feb.–May 1885, on Granville's instructions, in unsuccessfully attempting to induce the Pope to reject Walsh in favour of a more moderate candidate for the see of Dublin, was himself the subject of attack from the radical ministers, who loudly demanded his recall (in April) and denounced his claims to a baronetcy (in June), with the object of inducing the hierarchy to promote a radical-Irish entente.

[2] *The Times*, 25 July 1885, p. 9.

[3] For Chamberlain's private view of Spencer at this time, and his advice to a young Liberal member to follow his and Dilke's example by not attending the dinner to him, see G. W. E. Russell, *Fifteen Chapters of Autobiography* (first published as *One Look Back*), London 1912, p. 271. Russell did in fact attend the dinner (Rosebery's journal 24 July).

[4] As time passed, the Liberals increasingly related their possibly fortuitous and certainly not definitive defeat on 9 June 1885 to a general rearrangement of parties brought about by conspiratorial negotiations between the Conservatives and the Irish. They traced the origin of the alliance to the Soudan vote of censure in Feb. 1885, when the Irish voted *en bloc* with the Tories, and saw in the attitude of the caretaker ministry to Irish affairs clear signs of payment for services rendered. Finally, in June 1886 Parnell publicly revealed the details of his secret interview with Carnarvon on 1 Aug. 1885.

The Liberals overestimated the part played by secret negotiations in determining the existence and attitudes of Salisbury's ministry, but they did not guess, then or later, at the extent to which the other two parties talked over quite secondary matters of tactics and arrangements. There were two distinct phases. In Feb. 1885, with Churchill abroad, there was already a dialogue going on (Rowland Winn, Tory chief whip to Salisbury, 2 Mar. 1885, enclosing memorandum dated 27 Feb. 1885 'of interview this day with Mr Parnell'.) A second agreement was worked out after Salisbury was invited to take office. Parnell was given the

assured him they would accept. Emly told me lately that he once had a conversation with Chamberlain at dinner, somewhere, having hardly any acquaintance with him, and Chamberlain told him his political programme, which he and his friends would act upon *whenever Gladstone had retired—not until then.* Its principle *was abolition of privilege—no Established Church, no House of Lords, a single Chamber, etc.* 'We shall be defeated in the first campaign', he said, 'but at the end of five years we shall carry it all.'

I remember at one of the Committees[1] at Spencer House I said that the Irish did not object to 'special legislation' in the case of the Church Act. Oh! he said, that legislation will very soon take place here in England.

Walked to Hill St. Strange to walk through scores of women silently offering their bodies to the passer-by. How often have I done it, without speaking a word to any of them since the year 1851.

Wednesday 29 July. . . . There is a great piece of scandal, which looks like truth, about Dilke[2]—and which I heard from H. Grenfell, then from May and Mundella. The lady is a Mrs

---

Chief Secretary of his choice and some minor Irish legislation. (Memorandum in Winn's hand following a meeting with Power, the Irish Whip, 20 June 1885, Salisbury MSS.) Besides the chief whip and Carnarvon, Churchill had his own dealings with the Nationalists. His papers at Churchill College, Cambridge only give indirect glimpses of this (e.g. Churchill MSS. x. 1177, and xiii. 1526). Later, however, he confided to his closest friend, Henry James: 'I wondered constantly at [Parnell] remaining silent in 1886 . . . He was several times at my house (No. 2 Connaught Place) during the summer of 1885, and we arranged a great many things in connection with the General Election of that year, the most perfect confidence between us. When I went to Ulster and attacked the Parnellites all round, I fully expected that Parnell would disclose our conversations, but he never uttered a word, and has never done so since.' (James MSS.) The true picture is not the Liberal version—that there was an overreaching strategic alliance of which particular actions were only symptoms—but rather of a multiplicity of independent and indeed competitive attempts to reach joint solutions of limited problems, without going into questions of strategy.

[1] i.e. the *ad hoc* Irish committee of Cabinet which met in May 1885.

[2] Mrs Crawford's initial confession to her husband was made on Friday, 17 July, reaching Dilke's ears that weekend (Roy Jenkins, *Sir Charles Dilke*, p. 217). Lord Cranbrook's diary for 29 July also mentions 'these rumours, of which the air is full', which he had discussed with Lord and Lady Iddesleigh. The rumour was recorded in Rosebery's journal as early as 20 July.

Crawford, a young married woman, daughter of Eustace Smith, M.P.,¹ sister of Mrs Ashton Dilke.—Dilke has gone away on plea of health.

Thursday 30 July. . . . A good deal of talk with Clermont after dinner—we got upon Gladstone—and his treatment of me last autumn. Clermont said 'it showed the truth of what Frances² said, that he wasn't a gentleman.'

Friday 31 July. . . . Luncheon with Lady Molesworth—Miss Helen Henniker³ and Gillett⁴ there. They talked of the Dilke affair—said Crawfords to be hushed up by payment of £25,000! and also of a fracas about Mrs Langtry between Lord Lonsdale and Sir George Chetwynd.⁵ Miss Henniker's talk showed Conservative dissatisfaction with some of the Govt arrangements. She said that Lord Salisbury was lazy, and allowed others to have their way. There is a remarkable article in the *Standard*⁶ beginning

¹ M.P. (Lib.) for Tynemouth since 1868.
² Frances, Lady Waldegrave. For evidence of her pronounced disesteem for Gladstone (in 1870–8) see O. Wyndham Hewett, *Strawberry Fair* (London, 1956), pp. 207, 209, 231, 256.
³ Hon. Helen Henniker (d. 1907), d. of 4th Baron Henniker: her uncle, Sir E. Kerrison, was a prominent Tory backbencher 1852–67.
⁴ Probably Maj. William Gillett (1839–1925), banker, soldier, traveller: co-founder, Bachelors' Club 1881; published several polemical books in support of Conservative party.
⁵ On 20 July these two gentlemen had a free fight in Hyde Park over a photograph of Mrs Langtry (Rosebery's journal, 20 July). 'Don't meddle with my Lily' Chetwynd said, attacking Lonsdale with a whip (Douglas Sutherland, *The Yellow Earl*, London, 1965, pp. 71–2).
⁶ See *The Standard*, 31 July 1885, p. 4, where the first leader is an extraordinarily bitter attack on Churchill. This paper, despite Salisbury's denials, was believed to reflect Salisbury's views on occasion, through his associate Alfred Austin, its chief writer on foreign affairs. Churchill himself believed that Salisbury had instigated the article referred to above, and it took a tactful letter from Beach, saying Salisbury was incapable of such an attack, to restore harmony (Beach to Churchill, 17 Aug. 1885, Churchill MSS. vii. 809). Later Churchill came to ascribe obvious leaks in the *Standard* to Lady Salisbury, whom he called 'Ashmead-Bartlett in petticoats', the comparison being with an incurably insensitive and bigoted Tory backbencher. (R. Brett's journal, 26 Dec. 1886, Esher MSS.) A possible reason for the Press attack may be found in an otherwise unsupported

'It is time to speak out' and protesting against Randolph Churchill
—'overrated man', 'doing irreparable mischief to the party'.

Wednesday 5 August. . . . Luncheon with Gregory[1]—just from
Ireland. His rents well paid, but he hopes he may be able to sell his
estates to his tenants.—He had just met John Morley, who said
that Gladstone must go on, and form another Govt—otherwise
the Liberal party would break up. Gregory is a friend of Mrs
Eustace Smith,[2] and takes the worst view of Dilke.
    . . . Dined Brooks's. . . . Henry James fears the Dilke affair must
come into the Divorce Court. The lady has withdrawn her confession, made, she says, in irritation, because her husband pressed
her about an anonymous letter.

Friday 7 August. . . . Long talk about my affairs, which have never
been so bad. He [the agent] does not know how to meet the
instalments of legacies now due, or how to carry on the sinking—
the former difficulty caused by nonpayment of rents and of sums
due by dealers for coal.

Tuesday 11 August. To Radstock early. Took an interesting walk
with McMurtrie. . . . I told him I did not expect to be invited to
take office again.

Sunday 23 August. . . . Met Mr Young[3] in the churchyard and
talked—His sermons today lamentable—certainly poor specimens
of popular Christianity[4] with all its irrational and unmoral con-
fusions.—Now and then I ask myself whether it is honest for me
to go to church. Yet to stay away would be a real loss to me, and

story told by Cadogan to Rosebery a year later, to the effect that Salisbury had
been peremptorily overruled at the Cabinet of 20 July 1885 by Churchill *et al.*
about suspending the National League, an action which Salisbury 'then declared
he would not forgive' (Rosebery's journal, 28 July 1886).

[1] For Gregory, see above, 21 Jan.
[2] Mother of Mrs Crawford.
[3] Rev. Charles Young, ordained 1859: vicar of St Mary's, Brighton 1859–85;
appointed vicar of Chewton Mendip with Emborough, 1885.
[4] Cf. entries for 11 Jan. and 18 Oct.

would not express my true feeling. Very despondent. My love my love!

Saturday 29 August. . . . Eddie Strachey met H. Fowler M.P.[1] today, who spoke with no great confidence of the result of the elections.—Eddie has heard that Chamberlain says that neither Granville nor Northbrook shall be in the next Liberal Govt. Fowler told him that Chamberlain had not allowed Disestablishment to be made a test question at these elections—also that Hartington was going to make a most important declaration about Ireland. Fowler speaks strongly against Parnell and any alliance with him.

Monday 31 August. . . . Hartington made an important speech on Saturday[2]—very decided against Parnell—also, without naming him, against Chamberlain's land schemes.

Thursday 3 September. . . . Took Essex and general accounts. I am managing these estates for the purpose of paying about £17,000 a year to other people, and this after the sale of Strawberry Hill.

Friday 4 September. . . . Read political articles etc. in the *Nineteenth Century.* Parnell has defied Hartington at a dinner[3] at the Dublin Mansion House, where they drank 'Ireland a Nation' and not the Queen.

Shall I take any part in political events and struggles which lie before us? I feel no spirit for it.

Sunday 13 September. . . . Read Lessing's essay, *Leibnitz von den Ewigen Strafen,* (I had read it in 1850), Feuerbach's *Essence of Christianity* (the Marian Evans translation),[4] Farrer, etc. Have

---

[1] Henry Fowler (1830–1911): M.P. (Lib.) Wolverhampton 1880–1908; leading Methodist; Under-Sec. at Home Office 1884–5 and Financial Secretary to Treasury 1885–6; in Cabinet 1892–5 and 1905–10.

[2] *The Times,* 31 Aug. 1885, p. 8: speech at Waterfoot, Lancs.

[3] *The Times,* 2 Sept. 1885, p. 6.

[4] Marian Evans, *Ludwig Feuerbach's Essence of Christianity* (1854), the only book to appear under 'George Eliot's' real name.

never read anything more unintelligible than Feuerbach's first chapter.

Friday 18 September. . . . The papers have been full of late of the relations of the sexes[1]—much that is false and corrupt exposed and condemned—and yet I feel a great deal of the preaching against 'impurity' to be unnatural.

. . . I have no hold on the press or public, and am not able to take part in the public discussion of politics.

Saturday 19 September. . . . Found Gladstone's manifesto in the *Pall Mall*,[2] with an article on it headed—An Old Man's Programme. It is a very long address to Midlothian. He offers himself for election, but leaves it doubtful whether he would form another administration. The address is moderate, not exciting or inspiring.

Sunday 20 September. . . . I have been carefully reading and marking Mr G's manifesto. It is very skilful, and must have a great effect in keeping the party together—What power he has! what influence over public opinion and action!—generally well used.

Saturday 26 September. . . . Chamberlain declares[3] that he will not take office[4] in a Liberal Cabinet which does not adopt his three

---

[1] A reference to the campaign, initiated by W. T. Stead in the *Pall Mall Gazette* and widely taken up, against various forms of commercial vice. The campaign, which ultimately landed Stead in jail, was linked with the passage of the Criminal Law Amendment Act, 1885, which *inter alia* raised the age of consent. In the course of his inquiries into the 'Maiden Tribute' Stead came across the tracks of Gladstone and the Prince of Wales—or so Labouchere told people in the Lobbies. Reginald Brett, when writing to Stead begging him not to smear the good name of the ruling class, so misunderstood the position as to add 'Please do not think that I am concerned to defend the Prince of Wales or Mr G . . .' (Brett's journal, Esher MSS: 15 July 1885).   [2] For text, see *The Times*, 19 Sept. 1885, p. 8.

[3] In a speech at the Victoria Theatre, Lambeth, reported in *The Times*, 25 Sept. p. 7.

[4] Chamberlain's key words were 'It would be dishonourable in me, and lowering the high tone which ought to be observed in public life, if, after having committed myself personally as I have done to the advocacy of those proposals, I were to take any place in any government which excluded them from its programme.'

points: 1. Adjustment of taxation in favour of the poor. 2. Free Education. 3. Compulsory purchase of land by local authorities to create small proprietors.

Sunday 27 September. . . . I have been thinking of the refusal of the *Times* to print my speech. That kind of speech is wasted when not allowed to reach the public. There is no use in my making such. . . . It probably means that the newspaper people consider me gone by, on the shelf. I am sure that Gladstone's treatment of me this time last year greatly damaged me.

Wednesday 30 September. A friendly letter from Northbrook asking me to Stratton, and to talk Irish affairs. . . . The accounts from South of Ireland are bad—boycotting increasing, and the tyranny of the League.

Sunday 4 October. . . . I have been miserable—sunk in desolation—troubled and restless because I don't know what the life is that lies before me. H. Grenfell writes from Liverpool that George Melly[1]

The key term here, 'excluded', is ambiguous. Chamberlain later argued that he was not insisting that the points be *included*. Cf. 'I claimed that they should not be negatived in anticipation but I did not demand that they should be immediately adopted.' (Chamberlain to Morley, 22 Feb. 1890, printed in Chamberlain's *A Political Memoir, 1880–92*, ed. C. H. D. Howard, p. 301.) Carlingford's summary is otherwise unexceptionable.

Goschen spotted Chamberlain's concealed way of retreat: 'I read his declaration differently from the press. He will not stand aside, simply if his three points are not *included*, but only if they are specifically excluded.' (Goschen to A. Grey, 26 Sept.: Grey MSS.)

Nevertheless, despite his subsequent disavowal in 1890, and despite Goschen's correct instinct that Chamberlain had deliberately left room for backing down, Chamberlain did in fact say in private in autumn 1885 that his position was as Carlingford and the general public took it to be, i.e. that he required positive undertakings, not negative reassurances. His most specific private statement of his terms was (1) adjustment of taxation, as adequately dealt with in Gladstone's manifesto (2) Free Education to be 'an open question in the fullest sense' (3) local authorities with powers of compulsory purchase 'must come up as the first business undertaken . . . This is a *sine qua non*'. (Chamberlain to Harcourt, 9 Oct. 1885: Chamberlain MSS. JC 5/38/145.) Cf. similar letters to Dilke, 9 Oct. (JC 5/24/423), and to J. Morley, 21 Sept. (JC 5/54/629).)

[1] George Melly (1830–94): M.P. (Lib.) Stoke 1868–74; Liverpool merchant from 1859 till death.

tells him it is understood that I shall not be a candidate for office again—so also Selborne and Childers. My love my love!

Wednesday 7 October. . . . McMurtrie came to luncheon. . . . Much talk about my affairs. His chief hope lies in a restoration of the colliery income (by better times and the new seams) to its old amount, say £12,000 instead of £6,000 or £7,000. But I see no prospect of an income, on account of the weight of the bond debts—and I must be dependent on Clermont,[1] which is painful. How little my darling dreamed of such a situation as this!

Thursday 8 October. . . . I looked at our old house and felt the contrast with a sinking and sickness of heart. Now that I have lost Hamilton Place[2] and have scarcely any income, the material worldly contrast is greater than ever—my love my love!

Friday 9 October. [In Ireland.] . . . I felt on landing in Ireland as if it were a foreign and an enemy country—the very air seems charged with hostility and hatred towards England, and towards Irishmen also of my class—and yet I have a real feeling for the country.

Thursday 15 October. . . . My eyes are weak and painful.

Friday 16 October. . . . Read Mill: my eyes are in bad order.

Sunday 18 October. . . . Read Blunt's *Dictionary of Sects*, and Mill on Hamilton.[3] Nothing can be more melancholy than the history of Christian theology, except indeed that of the atrocious persecutions of heretics. What would Our Lord have thought of it all, if he could have foreseen it! Blunt talks of 'rationalism' as if it were a transient delusion of the human mind.

Friday 23 October. [In Ireland.] Heard . . . that my Red House tenants had come to [the agent] in Ardee in a body and refused to pay rent unless they got an abatement. . . . We discussed the

---

[1] See also entries under 1 Apr. and 24 Oct.

[2] The London house lent him while in office by Lord Northbrook.

[3] John Stuart Mill, *An Examination of Sir William Hamilton's Philosophy*, etc. (London, 1865.)

conduct of the tenants, which is unreasonable, and no doubt dictated by the local League. They were able and ready to pay their rent, but on hearing of Clermont's abatement agreed to demand the same. Their rents are notoriously low, they do not depend upon cattle, and there seems no reason for an abatement. So we decided to refuse. *Hale, the Protestant miller, was put forward.* He told [the agent] that he would pay *if he was served with a writ*, but that if he had not joined the rest his mill would have been boycotted. The tenants on W. Ruxton's[1] estate and others, with rents higher than mine, have paid in full.

Saturday 24 October. Some talk with Clermont. He had asked me whether I should like to have his half-yearly payments in advance, but I did not think it necessary to go into the question of what his allowance to me was to be, a subject which I hate.

. . . [In Dublin.] Sir P. Keenan[2] showed me how the Irish Endowed Schools Bill[3] had been altered in the H. of C.—the

---

[1] William Ruxton (1823–95) of Ardee House, co. Louth: in 1885 owned 2,262 acres, of annual value £2,279. Carlingford was distantly related to the Ruxton family, through a cadet branch from which he had inherited property.

[2] Sir Patrick Joseph Keenan (1824–94), civil servant: Inspector of National Education, Ireland, 1848; Head Inspector, 1854–9, Chairman of Inspection, 1859–71; Resident Commissioner of National Education, 1871–94; K.C.M.G. 1881; P.C. (I.) 1885. Keenan was described by an exceptionally well-informed source as follows: 'In religion a Roman Catholic. In politics a whig. He is Resident Commissioner and is virtually ruler of the Board' (George Fottrell, Dublin solicitor, to Chamberlain, 3 July 1885: Chamberlain MSS. JC 8/4/1/5).

[3] Educational Endowments (Ireland) Act, 1885, 48 & 49 Vict. c. 78: for an inside account of its passage, see 'Ireland and Party Politics 1885–7: An Unpublished Conservative Memoir (1)', *Irish Historical Studies*, xvi (1968), 161–2. The original bill, dropped on the change of government in June 1885, was re-drafted by Fitzgibbon in one day (7–8 Aug.) in time to become law on the last day of the session (14 Aug.). The Cabinet were indifferent or hostile to the measure, but Fitzgibbon obtained the willing help of Churchill and Holmes, the Irish Attorney-General, in passing what was essentially a 'judge-made law'. The Commission set up by the Act sat, under Fitzgibbon's chairmanship, until 1897 and rearranged endowments of £140,000 annual value in 1500 schools. In autumn 1885 the Act nearly became a dead letter because the hierarchy, like Carlingford, took it to have a Protestant bias. Significantly, it needed a persuasive letter from Churchill, emphasizing the pro-Catholic implications of Conservative policy on Irish education, to iron out the difficulties (Churchill MSS. viii. 974).

amendments devised by Lord Justice Fitzgibbon[1] in Protestant interests. He thinks there is 'a panic in England' about Home Rule and that there is likely to be an unnecessary surrender. Cross (Sir R.)[2] talked in that sense as of a thing inevitable.[3] Bishop Donnelly told him that it would come in a year, Archbishop Walsh said in two. Keenan thinks an elected Council in Dublin 'madness'.

Sunday 25 October. . . . Talked to Cumin. He had just seen Forster and thought badly of him—Said Mundella had been converted to 'Free Education' 'in half an hour'! They are sending M. Arnold to inquire into its working on the Continent. School *attendance* now better in England than in any other country. Cumin says they have difficult questions about R. Catholic schools.

Thursday 29 October. To our grave before luncheon. I read lately in my last year's diary the saying of Dr. Clarke,[4] when he heard of my darling's death, 'She has been *sacrificed*—Why didn't they send for me?' God help me! I suffer—I suffer—and justly.

---

[1] Gerald Fitzgibbon (1837–1909): Sol.-Gen. for Ireland 1877–8; app. Lord Justice of Appeal 1878; as judge continued his political activities behind the scenes: played host to meetings of English politicians with Irish conservatives; since 1876, in close contact, convivial and sometimes conspiratorial, with Churchill; during 1885–6 a regular and lengthy correspondence was kept up, though only Fitzgibbon's letters survive; his advice most heeded on Irish educational policy; often charged with changing his party abruptly on formation of 1874 government; a prominent member of the Church of Ireland.

[2] Sir Richard Assheton Cross (1823–1914): M.P. (Cons.), 1857–62, 1868–86; educ. Rugby and Trinity Coll., Cambridge; bar 1849; Home Sec. 1874–80, 1885–6; cr. Viscount 1886; Indian Sec. 1886–92; Privy Seal 1895–1900; friend and adviser of the Queen for many years; bibulous in later life.

[3] Though most letters to and from Cross at this period have disappeared, it is unlikely that he ever put forward the view here attributed to him as a factor which should influence policy. Indeed Cross, on the available evidence, expressed no opinion at all about Ireland until very near the fall of the Conservative government, when he wrote a long letter to Salisbury demanding 'a determined statement in clear and unmistakeable language' declaring Conservative opposition to any form of devolution. (Cross to Salisbury, 16 Jan. 1886: Salisbury MSS.) Keenan probably derived his knowledge of Cross' defeatism from his fellow official Jenkinson, since Cross and Jenkinson did meet briefly at this time.

[4] 'Clarke' was in fact none other than Sir Andrew Clark (1826–93), best known as Gladstone's doctor. In 1879 he was called to Lady Waldegrave and arrived an hour before she died, a matter for which Carlingford blamed himself

Saturday 31 October. [At Stratton, Hants.] . . . A good deal of talk with Northbrook, especially about Ireland. His cousin Jenkinson[1] has made up his mind that Home Rule or Repeal must be given. Sat with Northbrook and Henry Grenfell after the ladies went to bed.

My speech is not mentioned in *The Times* . . . and shortly and very imperfectly reported in the Bath papers—so much for my trouble and torment. I ought to have said less, and about Ireland only.

Sunday 1 November. . . . I have been reading of the friendships of Grimm and Diderot etc.—amusing to contrast them with my British friends.

Monday 2 November. [At Stratton, Hants.] . . . Walked with Northbrook through the woods. Talk about Gladstone and the political situation etc. He said he did not wish for office—did not think it would be satisfactory—doubted whether Hartington and Chamberlain could act together about Ireland. He has refused all invitations to speak.[2] My speaking has been utter failure so far as my interests or credit are concerned, especially my Bath speech. The newspapers have ignored me—but I have the satisfaction of

---

too harshly, as she had refused to take her condition seriously and had relied on a local doctor till within two days of her death.

[1] Edward George Jenkinson (1836–1919), Irish civil servant: educ. Harrow and Haileybury; entered Indian civil service in 1856, serving through the Mutiny; retired, 1880, as divisional commissioner in Oudh; selected by Spencer, 1882, to be his asst. private sec. at Dublin Castle 1882–4; Under-Sec. with responsibility for Police and Crime in Ireland, 1884–6; after a prolonged inter-departmental dispute, transferred to Home Office in London, Jan. 1886; in June 1886 was official responsible for Chamberlain's safety (Chamberlain MSS JC 8/9/1/7); probably only distantly related to Northbrook; C.B. 1883, K.C.B. 1888. For further statements of his Home Rule leanings, see G. E. Buckle, ed., *The Letters of Queen Victoria, 1862–85*, iii. 610 (Ponsonby to the Queen, 9 Dec. 1885, reporting Jenkinson's view of Home Rule as a potentially conservative measure); Askwith, *Lord James*, p. 157; and, most usefully, a series of letters from him to Spencer, 20 Dec. 1885–29 Jan. 1886, Spencer MSS., arguing against any precipitate declaration for Home Rule, and for prior settlement of the land question.

[2] Palmer's *Index to The Times* records no speeches out of doors by Northbrook in the second half of 1885.

not having given way to cowardice or indolence. We discussed Mr G. (whom Northbrook does not love), Dilke, Chamberlain, etc. We went to his room and he showed me statements of his rents etc.[1]

Tuesday 3 November. Left Stratton at 9.30, as they were assembling for prayers—glad to get away, not feeling fit for society.

Friday 6 November. Read arrears of newspapers, and Hartington's speeches[2] just made at Belfast—very good—satisfactory to my mind, if I understand him.

Monday 9 November. . . . I am called upon to pay £1,000 to a Revd. John Hamilton,[3] part of a sum borrowed by Chi[4] from 'Alek. Hamilton' for my darling—I am so dreadfully weak in my finances that any call of this kind is embarrassing.

[At a Somerset election meeting.] Eddie [the Liberal candidate] is ready at answering. He and McMurtrie were strong for 'free education'. I said I could not commit myself to it. Said also that I should not have taken the chair if the candidate had declared for Disestablishment. I also said that I could not have supported him, if he had coquetted with Home Rule.

Tuesday 10 November. . . . Read a mass of speeches—one by Mr G. at Edinburgh,[5] which seems to contain an intention to give Home Rule.

Wednesday 11 November. . . . Read again Hartington's Belfast speech—the best that has been made on the Nationalist demands—

[1] See below (p. 144) 'Miscellaneous Jottings', no. 1.

[2] See *The Times*, 6 Nov. 1885, p. 6.

[3] A Church of Ireland clergyman, ordained 1837: rector of Annaghdown, co. Galway, from 1876.

[4] Chichester Hamilton (1835–79), nephew of Carlingford by his sister Mrs Hamilton, widowed 1861. 'Chi' for some years managed Carlingford's (and Lady Waldegrave's) estates, but gave this up on becoming ill in 1876.

[5] Speech given on arrival at Edinburgh, 9 Nov., cited in *Annual Register*, 1885, p. 176, but not reported by *The Times*.

Parnell scoffs at him, and speaks of Gladstone's words in Edinburgh as the most important for Ireland ever uttered by an Englishman.[1]

Thursday 12 November. . . . Read new reviews, and Barry O'Brien's *Fifty Years of Concessions to Ireland*[2]—as usual my name is scarcely mentioned—no sign that I had anything to do with the Irish Land Acts, or Liberal policy towards Ireland. How indignant my own queen of a woman would have been!

Henry Grenfell writes that he hears from Trevelyan that the 'Irish Intransigents' suspend all violence to enable Parnell to return all his members, and give him a year to do what he can in parliament. Ireland full of Irish Americans and American money—and organized for violent action (assassination?).

Callan[3] has been rejected by Parnell and the League.

[1] See *Annual Register*, 1885, p. 178, on Parnell's speech at Liverpool on 10 Nov., the key phrase above being virtually accurate.

[2] R. Barry O'Brien, *Fifty Years of Concessions to Ireland, 1831–1881* (London, 1883). A second volume appeared in 1885.

[3] Philip Callan, M.P. Dundalk 1868–80, co. Louth 1880–5: defeated Carlingford in co. Louth election, 1874, but elected to sit for Dundalk: seconded the motion to set up the Home Rule League, 1873: a genuine Nationalist who cooperated periodically with Parnell but never fully accepted his authority. Callan's loyalty to Butt having led him to say ugly things about the Parnellites, Parnell in 1880 helped Russell (subsequently attorney-general and lord chief justice), defeat Callan at Dundalk, but Callan was returned for Louth in spite of him. In 1880–5 the Parnellites found Callan's drunken indiscretions provocative and harmful, though Gladstone thought him the wittiest speaker on the Irish side. In 1885 Callan was refused an official nomination at Louth,which he however contested despite an alleged Parnellite offer of a nomination in the North. The very bitter contest at Louth led to lurid rumours about dealings between Parnell and extremist factions (Albert Grey to Lady Mary Ponsonby, 20 Dec. 1885, in *Mary Ponsonby, A Memoir, Some Letters, and a Journal*, ed. Magdalen Ponsonby, London 1927, pp. 172–3). Callan did not take his repudiation lying down, and attempted to create a purely personal Tory-Irish alliance. He solicited written support from Lord Randoph Churchill, 19 Nov. 1885: 'your opinion will do me great service with a large number of our 300 Conservatives at whose *private* meetings your letters will be read if you so permit' (Churchill MSS. ix, 1076). Following his defeat, an Ulster Tory M.P., McKane, put up £1000 to enable Callan to make an election petition (Jan. 1886). Callan at this time claimed 'he had a case which will put Parnell into gaol, and keep him out of parliament for seven years', but McKane's sudden death (11 Jan. 1886) enabled the Parnellites to contend that the petition was technically invalid (Albert Grey to third earl Grey, 15 Jan. 1886, Grey MSS. Durham Univ.)

Monday 16 November. Constance went home ... she is very anxious that I should not be abroad when a Liberal Govt is formed again—but I do not believe that I shall be concerned in that.

Tuesday 17 November. ... When I bid McMurtrie goodbye and said I did not expect to have any part in the next Liberal Govt, he was positive that I should be offered office, curiously so.

Friday 20 November. A very busy day. ... To Cook's for tickets. Then to the Bank of England and had a talk with Henry Grenfell. Said he heard that Salisbury fully intended to meet Parliament, that it would probably be a short Parliament,—that Salisbury held his party to be stronger than any other, treating the Liberals and Radicals as separate parties, which he has no right to do yet.

    ... [Henry Grenfell and Lady Sophia Macnamara][1] ... talked about Dilke today—said it wasn't safe for a woman to be in a room alone with him. For a year and half he had taken a devout turn, gone constantly to church, received the sacrament, etc.— curious piece of human nature.[2]

Cardinal Manning for his part tried to persuade Churchill to find Callan a post in India (Manning to Churchill, 11 Jan. 1886, Churchill MSS. xii, 1277). Callan's son became private secretary to the Unionist lord-lieutenant, Lord Dudley. For a not wholly accurate account of the Parnell-Callan quarrel, see Andrew J. Kettle, *Material for Victory* (Dublin, 1958), pp. 67–8.

  [1] Daughter of 3rd Earl of Listowel: m. 1854 Arthur Macnamara of Leighton Buzzard; Hon. Lady of the Bedchamber to H.R.H. Princess Louise, Marchioness of Lorne.

  [2] On 20 Feb. 1885 Dilke had mentioned (during a Cabinet!) the subject of religion to Chamberlain for the first time in his life, describing himself as a Positivist, but going on to affirm his 'very strong belief in Christ's moral teaching'. However, the following year Dilke wrote to Chamberlain (11 July 1886: Chamberlain MSS. JC 5/24/188) in a much more definite manner. Dilke's letter of 11 July, of which only the letterhead survives, bears a note by Chamberlain's secretary 'This letter from Sir C. Dilke was destroyed by Mr Chamberlain on May 28 1912' but above the address there is a summary of the contents 're Crawford case—reading for orders'. However in 1886, Chamberlain had been less concerned about concealing his friend's aberration, for on 14 July 1886 he wrote to Henry James 'I had a queer letter from Dilke on Monday. He is thinking of taking orders!' (James MSS.)

[On Saturday 21 November, Carlingford left London for San Remo, on a visit to Edward Lear. While there, already feeling deeply depressed, he was taken seriously ill, probably with a severe chill or pneumonia. He wrote later, 'I never was really ill before' and 'I can hardly fancy anyone feeling more ill and dejected and prostrated.' His illness began on 30 November, and his temperature was not normal again till 9 December. He was not able to correspond till 17 December, and subsequently had several relapses. His company was virtually confined to his man-servant and Edward Lear, and he maintained little contact with affairs in England. His only informant in the political world seems to have been Northbrook. More than ever *hors de combat* politically, he finished the year a lonely convalescent in Italy.]

Thursday 17 December. . . . I am constantly thinking of this terrible Irish problem. Shall I ever have to do with office again? It will be a blessing when that is decided, one way or another.

Wednesday 23 December. . . . An important letter from Hartington in the papers,[1] saying that he knows of no Home Rule proposal, and adheres to his speeches.

I am constantly thinking of this terrible Irish problem.

Low and weary today—with an uncomfortable head.

Northbrook has taken no notice of the letter written just after the fever left me, in answer to one from him, and telling him that I have been very ill. With him friendship has often to be matter of faith without evidence.

Thursday 24 December. . . . I wrote too hastily about Northbrook's silence—I have a long and interesting letter from him about the Irish question and Gladstone's conduct, of which Hartington and others with reason complain.

[1] See *The Times*, 21 Dec. 1885, p. 9 (leader on Hartington's letter) and p. 8 (text of Hartington's letter, dated 19 Dec., to Mr Brooks, chairman of his election com-mittee in Rossendale). Hartington's letter was drafted in concert with Goschen: see *The Letters of Queen Victoria, 1862–85*, iii, ed. G. E. Buckle (London, 1928), 715: Goschen to the Queen, 22 Dec. 1885. But cf. also Goschen to A. Grey, 20 Dec., Grey MSS.: 'I saw Hartington yesterday. He was not combative at all.'

Saturday 26 December. Troubled with the same swimming or light head. Dr H. thought it has to do with the nerves.

... Dr H. begs me to do as little writing or head work as possible—so have not written to Northbrook on the Irish question, or to O'Conor Morris,[1] from whom I have two letters.

Thursday 31 December. ... Awoke last night with the swimming and discomfort of head I had before. It keeps me awake, and I have it more or less all day today.

... Wrote to Northbrook. Told him I was decidedly for resistance to any Home Rule plan.

... This is how I have passed the last day of 1885.—God help me!

Miscellaneous jottings of uncertain date on blank pages of the 1885 journal.

1. *Memo. about landlord and tenant.* Northbrook is reducing his rents considerably, going back to the rental of about 20 years ago. He has spent largely on farms and cottages. His Stratton gross rent roll of about £7,000 a year is all spent on the house, grounds, gardens, and estate. He is the only landlord in that district who has no vacant farms. He knows a £500 a year farm for which the old landlord offered £100. This was refused, and it can't now be let for 6d. an acre. The Dean of Winchester[2] talked of a Chapter farm—old rent £1,200—actual rent £500. Alfred Seymour[3] has reduced his rents in Northamptonshire and Wiltshire fully 30 per cent. Spencer said last year that his rent receipts were less than they used to be by £8,000.

---

[1] William O'Conor Morris: educ. Epsom and Oriel; Irish Bar, 1854; Professor of Law at King's Inns; owned 2,000 acres in King's Co.; Irish County Court Judge from 1872; died 1904. Opposed to 1881 Irish Land Act as a landlord. Friend of Carlingford since 1869; wrote an autobiography, 1895.

[2] Very Revd. G. W. Kitchin, D.D. (1827–92).

[3] Alfred Seymour (1824–88), second son of Henry Seymour (M.P. Taunton 1826–30); his elder brother, H. D. Seymour, was M.P. Poole 1850–68, and a junior minister 1855–8. Alfred m. Isabella, widow of B. Botfield, M.P.; educ. Eton and Ch.Ch., Oxford, where he became a lifelong friend of Carlingford; M.P. (Lib.) Totnes 1863–8, Salisbury 1869–74; owned land in Som., Wilts., and Northants; his family became extinct and no papers have survived.

2. [At Balmoral.] Letter from Malet[1] to Granville, 23 May 1885. Conversation with Baron de Courcel, the French Ambassador. M. de Courcel said that Prince Bismarck was advising M. de Freycinet to be much more firm and *exigeant* towards England than he desired to be—and was not pleased at his reluctance to follow his (Prince Bismarck's) advice. M. de Freycinet believed Mr Gladstone to be sincere, and that by smoothing our path in Egypt he would promote an earlier retirement of our troops. Malet said that the object of Bismarck was transparent—he knew that as long as we remained in Egypt the old friendly relations between England and France were impossible. Conversation with Roumanian Minister . . . [who held] . . . since the Skierniewice interview Prince Bismarck had not concealed that Russia would renew her activity, but he had expected it to be directed against Persia and not England. [The Roumanian Minister] is convinced that at Skierniewice carte blanche was given to Russia to do what it liked in the East provided it renounced Slav propaganda in the countries where Austria desires to extend her influence. He said that Russia had now been checked by the unexpected firmness of England, but that we must not expect to remain quiet, and that she would probably next turn her attention to Persia.

3. I have heard two stories lately on a most interesting subject, the sexual relations of remarkable men and women. Eddie Strachey says that John Symonds[2] was told by a doctor who took part in, or knew all about the post mortem upon the body of Mrs Carlyle—he thinks it was Quin[3]—that she was found to be a virgin.

H. Grenfell was told the other day by Frederick Harrison[4] that he lived in great intimacy with G. H. Lewes and 'George Eliot' and that he was sure they never lived together as man and wife.

4. Letter[5] from Giers to Staal, circulated April 18 [1885]. Very bad.

---

[1] Ambassador at Berlin since Sept. 1884.

[2] John Addington Symonds (1807–71): M.D. 1828; physician and lecturer in medicine at Bristol 1831–69; Symonds' second daughter was Eddie Strachey's mother.

[3] Probably Frederic Hervey Foster Quin (1799–1878): founded the London homoeopathic hospital, 1850.

[4] Frederic Harrison (1831–1923), author, Positivist, and Liberal franc-tireur.

[5] See above, 18 Apr.

Assumes that the English officers directed the Afghan movement at Penjdeh—complains of the military escort which accompanied Lumsden, as encouraging the Afghans in hostility against Russia! It is under 500 men.

Telegrams from Chokir Pasha, Turkish Ambassador at Petersburg, to Grand Vizier, March 1885. Overtures of M. de Giers for a close alliance between Turkey and Russia. Russia would guarantee all territories of Turkey. Russia wishes to prepare 'un coup sévère' against England. In case of war desires to send her fleet into the Mediterranean. Letter of Grand Vizier to Sultan (through Private Secretary)—advises rejection of Russian offers, and an alliance with England. Turkey cannot be neutral.

5. From private letter[1] of Dufferin to Kimberley, Calcutta, 10 February 1885: '*Russian boundary proposals*—They are both impudent and outrageous, for instead of being a fair settlement, and in accordance with the natural features etc., they lift the Russians across the belt of desert which stretches from Sarakh to Khoja Saleh, and establish them in the fertile area which lies on the south of the desert, thus proving that their aim is not a defensible frontier for themselves but an advantageous base for future aggressions. ... The proper line, and the one which appears unassailable on legal and historical grounds (as might be presupposed from the physical conditions of the region) would be one drawn across the points where these gateways from north to south (the valleys of the Heri Rud, and Murghab) are the narrowest. This would give Pul-i-Khatun, Badghis, and Penjdeh to Afghanistan. Giers' proposals for the eastern-most portions of the line are still more monstrous. ... The location of Andkui on the west side of the line, is a shameless proceeding ...

'Now when we think that for years and years the Russians have been representing themselves as compelled by circumstances and much against their will to advance eastwards, it is too barefaced of them to endeavour in the face both of right and reason, to insist on filching these strips of territory from the Ameer. ... Whatever

---

[1] For the full text, the most relevant parts of which are accurately copied here, see the printed volume of Dufferin's correspondence with Kimberley: Dufferin MSS. D. 1071 H/M1/3, pp. 32–6.

settlement is reached will prove to our disadvantage. It is evident that no persuasion will induce Russia to accept a fair delimitation, i.e. the southern limit of the Kara Kum sands, which would correspond with a line drawn from Pul-i-Khatun to Khoja Saleh. But even if we can induce them to accept the line you have instructed Lumsden to determine, i.e. a compromise, . . . the result will be most unsatisfactory, for we shall have placed at Russia's disposal a large tract of highly fertile territory on this side of their natural frontiers, and have brought them so many miles nearer to Herat . . . and we shall have left the Ameer under the impression, not wholly unjustified, that we have deprived him of districts which we had already recognized as his, and which he had occupied with troops at our instigation. From all I can learn he is a man who will resent such a conclusion . . . bitterly. . . . But supposing we broke off negotiations, would this improve the situation? Most of my colleagues think it would. I very much doubt it. Even admitting, as I am quite ready to do, that the Russians would not respect the most formal treaty for any length of time it would put the drag on them!—violation of a written agreement would be an iniquitous act which the English people would understand and might resent.'

Dufferin then points out the disadvantages of merely 'delimiting the boundary ourselves'. 'Any settlement with Russia' better than none at all. 'Given a little time' Heraut [sic] might be fortified, position in Europe improved, Egyptian imbroglio got rid of—preparations on our north west frontier advanced. 'Once comfortably established in Herat' the Russians would 'choose the most likely pretender to the Afghan throne they could lay their hands on.' 'The cruelties of the present man (Abdurrahman) have made him innumerable enemies etc. etc.'

6. Despatch of Sir E. Thornton,[1] Jan. 10. 85.

'Mons. de Giers[2] has a good many bitter enemies and very few true friends. His Excy enjoys no social position, except that of his

---

[1] British Ambassador to Russia.
[2] Russian Minister of Foreign Affairs, April 1882–95: in effective control of Russian foreign office from the time of the Treaty of Berlin; a specialist in Central Asian questions.

office, and has no fortune. Count Ignatieff is one of his bitterest and most unscrupulous enemies. . . . The strongest opposition is also made to Mons. de Giers by the Minister of War, and all military men, whose ambitious views are thwarted by His Excy's peaceful policy. . . . He enjoys however the full confidence and support of the Emperor, who seems to have a great respect for His Excy's known honesty and upright character' (and approves of his policy of peace). 'His Excy's resignation would not improve our relations with Russia. . . . I see no one who would be so well disposed towards us or who would be willing or able to resist the pressure of those who long to take vengeance upon us for the humiliation (as they consider it) of the Treaty of Berlin.'

7. Rough notes (extracts) from long letter of Wolseley to Brett,[1] lent me by Hartington, dated Korti, 28.2.85.

'Two days *too late*—horrible words! seem to be the property of a Liberal Govt. I hear men on all sides say, 'Oh! if Mr Gladstone had only made up his mind a month earlier, we should be on our way down the Nile having relieved Gordon.' Our men did struggle like heroes—all in vain. Never had a General more brilliant prospects than those before me on New Year's Day. I felt confident that Gordon and Khartoum would be safe from the day that one or two steamers with a handful of British soldiers reached it. I had even sent a camel load of new red coats. Please think how nearly, how very nearly these plans succeeded, and perhaps you will be able to realize how I feel over this *too late* business. I still believe that if Stewart (Sir Herbert) had not been wounded Khartoum would have been saved. Wilson's (Sir Charles) nerve gave way completely—he was worse than useless for he demoralized them.—You look at these things from a party and political point of view. I feel as if someone had tapped my heart of its lifeblood when I think of the splendid soldiers I have lost to no purpose—what is a game of chess to you party men is life and death to me—Happy for you that you did not take the advice of

---

[1] Hon. Reginald Baliol Brett, s. of Lord Esher: private sec. (unpaid) to Hartington from 1877, until Mar. 1885; M.P. (Lib.) Falmouth, 1880–5; letter not printed in works on Hartington and Esher.

that silly man Sir A. Clarke[1] to go to Suakin—What then could have saved the Dongola province and the Wady Halfa frontier? You would have had the Arabs pressing on the Nile villages by this time, and Cairo itself in revolt. I am and always was against any active intervention in Egypt—I never believed in the importance of the Suez Canal—I believe we can no longer hold our own in the Mediterranean. Sailors whose opinion I value assure me of that. We must depend upon the Cape route. Any idiot will be able to block the Canal—the bombardment of Alexandria (?) cruel and silly—But we can't in honour leave Egypt until we have pacified the Soudan—If we do, the Mahdi will certainly reach Cairo. Give the Soudan to the Sultan—this not a noble policy, but we have no sound interests in Egypt—no one on our side—the Turks could not cross the 300 miles of desert from the Soudan— We ought to *clear out*, if possible.'[2]

[1] Career soldier in Royal Engineers: Inspector-General of Fortifications, 1882; dispatched to Cairo, 1882, to inquire into health of British forces in Egypt; a Liberal: a strong supporter of the Suakin route to Khartoum since Feb. 1884, when he had drawn up a memorandum for the Cabinet urging immediate construction of a Suakin-Berber railway. See Col. R. H. Vetch, *Life of Lt.-Gen. the Hon. Sir Andrew Clarke* (London, 1905), pp. 265–9.

[2] A reference to this letter may be found in *In Relief of Gordon: Lord Wolseley's Campaign Journal of the Khartoum Relief Expedition, 1884–5*, ed. Adrian Preston (London, 1967), pp. 161–2. Wolseley wrote on 7 Mar. 1885 'I wish I could see my way out of this Soudan business quickly, for with our small military resources I don't like the idea of having us tied down to military operations at this great distance from the seaboard, the duration or magnitude or extent of which I am unable to estimate. I wrote home by last post to Brett, pointing this out, and I hope he may show my letter to Hartington. What I recommend is coming to terms with Turkey and paying the Sultan well to take over this Soudan.'

Cf. also a note by E. Hamilton (diary, 1 Apr. 1885: B.M. Add. MS. 48639, ff. 118–20), referring to a gloomy letter from Wolseley (whether the one above is not clear), which had much shaken Hartington's confidence, not in the war, but in Wolseley. Hamilton summarized Wolseley's advice as 'Get out of the Soudan and even out of Egypt as soon as you can. Let the Turk into the Soudan ... Resign office sooner than lock your army up in that desert country ...'

Brett's harsh judgement, probably inspired by the above letter, is not unfair: 'It is astonishing how imprudent, for a prudent man in private and military affairs, Wolseley is upon paper. He seems incapable of writing with reserve or even with deliberation. It is impossible to suppose that he would adhere to everything he says in his letter to me. It is quite inconsistent with what he has said in his private letters, and with his telegrams to you.' (Brett to Hartington, 7 Apr. 1885: Esher MSS.)

[END OF JOURNAL]

APPENDIX
Carlingford and the Colonial Office in 1870

Memorandum by Chichester Fortescue
on his Claims to the Colonial Office, 1870

[The following memorandum,[1] printed here *in extenso*, stands on its own in Carlingford's papers and cannot be usefully related to his other correspondence. Its presence here is felt to be justified by the light it sheds on the ways of men and the problems of prime ministers. The document is unusual in its careful recording of the way politicians talk to each other about their central preoccupation—their position relative to each other—and the small change of the social manoeuvres associated with this.]

I was offered the Irish Office again, with seat in the Cabinet, by Mr Gladstone, on the evening of 5 Dec. 1868, at G. Glyn's[2] house in Berkeley Square. I said the Colonial Office was what I wished for, from long connexion,[3] etc. He said he was sure I would not press that subject, when he told me that he had offered Lord Granville his choice of offices, and he had chosen the C.O. He added 'Lord Clarendon's health is very far from strong, and, if he should prove unable to go on at the Foreign Office, we have an admirable Foreign Minister in Granville' I quite understood this to imply that if such a transfer should take place, the C.O. would fall to me, and I told Lady Walde-grave so, when I went home. It could have meant nothing else. It was intended to smooth my disappointment, and to hold out hopes for the future.

Lord Clarendon died on Monday morning, 27 June 1870. On Tuesday I called on Spencer at Spencer House, and told him that I should put in my claim for the C.O., that I had a very strong feeling about it, and that I did not think I should go on in office, if I were passed over. He strongly protested against such an idea—'Who could possibly be found for the Irish Office? etc.'—'not Monsell[4]—nobody he could think of'. Went to the C.O., and saw Lord Granville in the private secretary's room. After talking of the Land Bill in the Lords, I said 'You won't be surprised if I tell you that if you migrate from this place to the F.O., I shall renew my claim for the C.O. Will you tell Gladstone this?' He promised to do so. Very little more passed. He

[1] Strachie MSS., Strachie: Carlingford H. 326, Somerset County Record Office. In the text, certain abbreviations have been expanded for the sake of clarity.

[2] Liberal chief whip, 1868–73: subsequently 2nd Baron Wolverton.

[3] Fortescue had served as Under-Sec. for Colonies 1857–8 and 1859–65.

[4] A Catholic convert who served unsuccessfully as P.M.G. 1871–3: 1st Baron Emly.

asked further questions upon points in the Land Bill, and as I was leaving the room, said—'Then you wish me to tell Gladstone that you renew the claim to the C.O. which you put forward when the government was formed.' I said 'Yes—but much more strongly now.'

When I went back to the library of the House, I wrote to Granville as follows (not word for word):

'When you asked me just now whether you should tell Mr Gladstone that I wished now to renew my claim to the C.O., I ought to have said somewhat more than I did. The facts are these. When I accepted my present place, Mr Gladstone gave me reason to believe that I should not be a fixture at the Irish Office, if (by some process agreeable to yourself, *bien entendu*), the C.O. should become vacant during the term of his government. Since then I have been able to do the government some service during 2 sessions, and an arduous period of Irish affairs. I therefore now feel my claims for the C.O. to be very strong, indeed stronger than those of any other person. And what I desire is, that Mr Gladstone should make no arrangements for filling up that office, without hearing from myself my view of my own position with respect to it, in case I should be passed over upon the present occasion.'

The next day, having heard nothing, and seen a paragraph in the *Daily News* to the effect that Kimberley[1] was to have the C.O., I went to Lord Granville's. He was very cordial and said that he had told Gladstone at once what I had said to him, and sent him my letter. I said I could hardly think that Gladstone would fill up the C.O., without communicating with me, after what passed between us, when he formed his government. (He would have done so, however), and I told him what had passed then. After stating my claims, I added—'indeed I doubt whether I could go on at all, if I were passed over now'. He at once exhorted and entreated me not to use any such 'threat'. He said—'Now will you allow me to talk to you, exactly as I would to my brother Freddy, if he were sitting there?' I assented, of course. He then gave his advice, doing it very well. The upshot was—'You *have* very strong claims ("I must add that Gladstone also has claims upon you")—You are quite right to press them strongly, and make the best fight you can—but you must not threaten resignation. You can't carry into effect such a threat with any credit to yourself, etc.' I said I was telling him what my feeling was, but that I had been very cautious and silent with others. He said 'Will you promise me one thing—not to make up your mind on that subject, without first stating the case fully & fairly

---

[1] Kimberley was in fact appointed, July 1870, holding office till the ministry resigned in 1874. He was reappointed Colonial Sec. in 1880, again frustrating Carlingford's only specific political ambition.

to some friend in whose opinions you can trust, etc.' and he suggested Sir George Grey.[1]

I assented to this, & mentioned M. Van de Weyer.[2] I went back to Lady Waldegrave and then called on M. Van de Weyer. I had hardly sat down, when in came Lord Granville. As soon as he saw me, he said 'You mustn't suspect me'. He and Van de Weyer went for a very few minutes into the next room. I told M. Van de Weyer the whole story. Lady Waldegrave had told him the day before what had passed between Gladstone and myself, when he offered me the Irish Office. He had understood that he had given me a promise of the C.O. in case of a vacancy and had said that I ought to write to him at once and claim it. When he heard exactly what had been said on that occasion by Gladstone, he said 'well—there was a bit of diplomacy, but not more'. We talked a long time. He was clear that I should not threaten resignation, nor resign. He said that I should not be justified in leaving, the government—should not be doing the right thing—should make enemies of all my colleagues etc. *But*, he said, 'You will have a *grievance*, a very good thing to have'. When I said that I must not have it said of me that I was ready to submit to anything etc., he entirely denied that I was liable to any such imputation. He was most friendly and kind and greatly interested and gratified at being consulted. I told him I had promised Lord Granville to consult him. He said that he had come about another matter (a private dinner of Van de Weyer's for the Princess Louise) but that when he left him, he had said 'You will have serious matters to speak of with Fortescue'.

I called on Mr Gladstone the same evening (Wednesday) but, at his request, postponed the interview until the next morning.

We had a long conversation. He said that his letter to Lord Granville, written on reading mine to the latter, contained all he had to say about the matter.

I said I considered myself to have a stronger claim for the C.O. than any other person—founded on a long & exceptional connexion with the office (Cardwell's superseding me in the House of Commons, after I had long managed colonial business there,[3] not to be forgotten), from services rendered to his government in the Irish Office, and from the expectations held out to me by himself, when I took office. He fully

---

[1] Sir George Grey, Bt. (1799–1882): Liberal minister, who had retired from active leadership in 1866 but continued to play the part of a disinterested elder statesman.

[2] A former Belgian Ambassador, settled in England, where he was a respected social figure in his own right for reasons that are not very obvious.

[3] In Apr. 1864 Cardwell had succeeded the Duke of Newcastle as Colonial Sec., thus effectively taking away from Fortescue the role of chief spokesman on colonial affairs in the House of Commons which he had held for nearly five years.

admitted the value of the services I had performed in the Irish Office' but added that admirable service had been performed by several members of the government, indeed he did not know any government in which so much of such service had been found—and that this applied especially to one person who was not in the Cabinet, Forster.[1]

He said he was unable to agree that former connexion with a particular department, even a long one, in itself gave a man a claim to be the head of the department—he could not admit such a claim. If admitted at all, it could only be in the case of departments where some special knowledge or aptitude was required which was not the case with the C.O.—almost any member of the Cabinet would be fit for that office. (He hinted that even in the War office, the promotion of under-secretaries—de Grey[2] and Hartington—had not been very successful. But what had this to do with the argument?

As to expectations held out when I accepted the Irish Office, he would not admit any such intention. He did not question, though he said he did not recollect, his remark about Lord Clarendon's failing health, and that 'we had an admirable Foreign Secretary in that case, in Granville' but he did not admit my deduction.

I said I differed from him entirely as to what constituted a fair claim for a particular office, supposing sufficient service to have been rendered to a government by the person claiming—that the satisfaction of claims and the rewarding of services depended upon opportunity—that it was because such an opportunity had now occurred, that I pressed my claims, that such another would probably not occur again during his government, that if the vacancy had not been that of the C.O., I should have said nothing—that, at all events, I must make him understand that I could not consent to consider myself as a fixture at the Irish Office, and that he must not consider me as such—that family reasons of themselves would render that impossible, that I could not go on dragging Lady Waldegrave over to Dublin winter after winter. That, as to Forster, while I acknowledged his services, and thought he ought to be in the Cabinet, I must say that, if he were to be promoted to the C.O. instead of myself, I should resent such a proceeding.

I also asked him the meaning of certain expressions in his letter to Lord Granville. He said one expression meant there was a plan in embryo to get the Prince of Wales to Ireland, either by providing him with a residence there, to which Granville was disposed, or, which was his own idea, by making him viceroy, standing in the same sort of relation to the conduct of Government as the Queen does, in which

[1] Forster entered the Cabinet in July 1870 without any alteration in his position as Vice-President of the Council.

[2] Later Marquess of Ripon.

case the Chief Secretary, whether under the same or a different name, would be a still more important minister than he is now.

The other expression meant that if the only difficulty in the way of giving me the C.O. lay in my not being in the House of Lords there would be no difficulty whatever in making me peer, if I desired it.

He said that there was no question of giving Forster the Colonies. He said a great deal to the effect, that I had not yet completed my work in Ireland, that the Education question still remained, not the least difficult of the three, & c., that it was for me and not for him to judge what was best for my own reputation, but that his firm persuasion was that I should lose and not gain in that respect by any change of office at present. As to the future, he by no means wished to assume that I was to be a fixture at the Irish Office, that unfortunately a year seldom passed over a government without bringing changes, that I had a full right to consideration in case of such opportunities etc.[1]

As to reputation gained in the Irish Office, I reminded him that the very magnitude of the Irish questions had made them the Prime Minister's questions, & but very partially those of the Irish Secretary. He said he could not admit that (that as to the Land Bill I had identified myself with it, that the way in which I had worked it through Committee showed knowledge of the subject beyond anyone else, tact, temper, etc.) had been admirable and left nothing to be desired.

I said my services to the government in keeping the Irish party together were by no means confined to the House of Commons and reminded him of all Lady Waldegrave had done in Ireland etc., to which he assented (I told him of her conversations with the Prince of Wales about Ireland, and how he had said 'let me have first turn'—that is, before Arthur).[2] As I left him, I said 'You must remember this conversation—I shall no doubt remind you of it'. He said 'certainly'.

This referred to what he had said of future opportunities, and to the notice I had given him that he must not expect me to continue indefinitely at the Irish Office.

Soon after leaving Mr Gladstone I went to Lord Granville. He was excessively cordial—said he had had a visit on the subject from Clermont. (This was very nice on Clermont's part, knowing how he hates doing such things.)

I told him the substance of what had passed—He asked whether Kimberley or Halifax was to have the C.O. He asked what advice Van

[1] Within six months Bright's illness provided Fortescue with the opportunity he was looking for. Fortescue succeeded Bright at the Board of Trade, and Hartington replaced Fortescue in Ireland, in Dec. 1870.

[2] i.e. Prince Arthur, cr. Duke of Connaught, 24 May 1874, and regarded by the Queen as better fitted for a public position in Ireland than the Prince of Wales.

de Weyer had given (adding, to save his conscience, that he was going to him anyhow, but if he had not found me there, he must have prepared him for my coming). I said Van de Weyer was of opinion that I ought to have the C.O., and that if I were passed over, I had a right to complain—it was a grievance—but he had advised me to go on. He said 'Depend upon it, you have done the right thing.'

He said, before he took the F.O., Hammond[1] had told him that the work was nothing like what it had been when he was there in 1852.

A few days afterwards, Hammond told him that there was no difficulty except Greece, that he had never known things so smooth. The same afternoon, there arrived the telegram of the acceptance of the Throne of Spain by Prince Leopold of Hohenzollern!

It seems likely that Lord Granville contributed to my not getting the C.O. from his desire to have the assistance of Lord Halifax in the Lords.[2]

[1] Edmund Hammond, 1st Baron Hammond (1802–90): entered Foreign Office 1824; Perm. Under-Sec. 1854–73; Baron 1874.

[2] The point here is that by appointing Kimberley, who had held the office of Lord Privy Seal since 1868, it was possible to create a suitable vacancy to bring Halifax back into the Government. Halifax's counsel and reputation were certainly highly valued: in 1868 Gladstone had written to him offering him the Lord Lieutenancy with a seat in the Cabinet (Gladstone to Carlingford, 7 Dec. 1868).

LIST OF UNPUBLISHED SOURCES

The following manuscripts were consulted in preparing this edition of Lord Carlingford's journal. Quotations from some of the collections appear in the footnotes and introduction, with the kind permission of the individuals and institutions who now own them.

Cairns MSS. in the Public Record Office, London.

Chamberlain MSS. in Birmingham University Library.

Childers MSS. in the Royal Commonwealth Institute, London.

Churchill MSS. in Churchill College Library, Cambridge.

Cranbrook MSS. in the Ipswich and East Suffolk Record Office, Ipswich.

Devonshire MSS. at Chatsworth House, Derbyshire.

Dilke MSS. in the British Museum, London.

Dufferin MSS. in the Northern Ireland Public Record Office, Belfast.

Esher MSS. in Churchill College, Cambridge. (These papers are closed to inspection for the time being, but by a special arrangement the editors were allowed access to R. Brett's journal for 1885.)

Gladstone MSS. divided between the British Museum (referred to as the Gladstone Papers) and St Deiniol's Library, Hawarden, Flintshire (referred to as the Hawarden MSS.).

Granville MSS. in the Public Record Office, London.

Grey MSS. in Durham University Library.

Edward Hamilton MSS. in the British Museum.

James of Hereford MSS. (in private hands.)

Lothian MSS. in the Scottish Record Office, Edinburgh.

Mundella MSS. in Sheffield University Library.

Royal Archives, Windsor

Rosebery MSS. in the National Library of Scotland, Edinburgh.

Strachie MSS. in Somerset County Record Office, Taunton.

St Aldwyn MSS. in the Gloucestershire County Record Office, Gloucester.

Salisbury MSS. in Christ Church Library, Oxford.

Selborne MSS. at Lambeth Palace, London.

Spencer MSS. at Althorp Park, Northamptonshire.

Waldegrave MSS. at Chewton Mendip Priory, Somerset.

GENEALOGICAL TABLES

The Waldegrave and Strachey Families (simplified).

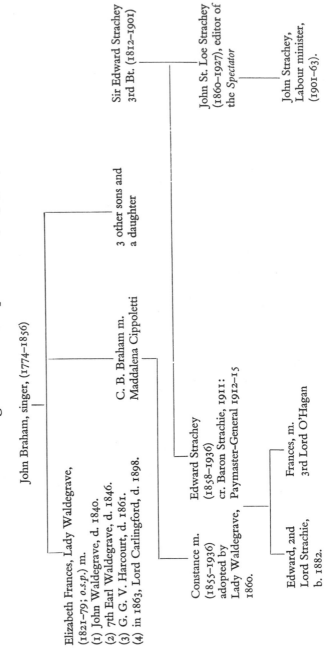

John Braham, singer, (1774–1856)

Elizabeth Frances, Lady Waldegrave,
(1821–79; o.s.p.) m.
(1) John Waldegrave, d. 1840.
(2) 7th Earl Waldegrave, d. 1846.
(3) G. G. V. Harcourt, d. 1861.
(4) in 1863, Lord Carlingford, d. 1898.

C. B. Braham m.
Maddalena Cippoletti

3 other sons and
a daughter

Sir Edward Strachey
3rd Bt. (1812–1901)

John St. Loe Strachey
(1860–1927), editor of
the *Spectator*

John Strachey,
Labour minister,
(1901–63).

Constance m.
(1855–1936)
adopted by
Lady Waldegrave,
1860.

Edward Strachey
(1858–1936)
cr. Baron Strachie, 1911:
Paymaster-General 1912–15

Edward, 2nd
Lord Strachie,
b. 1882.

Frances, m.
3rd Lord O'Hagan

The Fortescue Family (simplified).

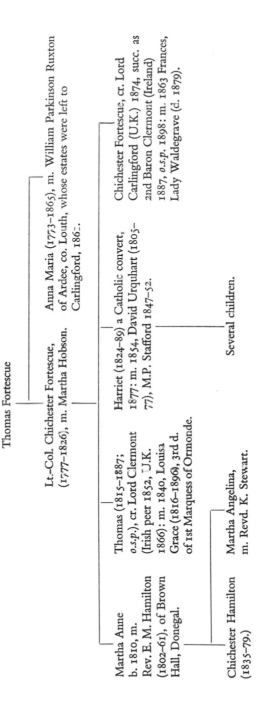

Thomas Fortescue

Lt.-Col. Chichester Fortescue, (1777–1826), m. Martha Hobson.

Anna Maria (1773–1865), m. William Parkinson Ruxton of Ardee, co. Louth, whose estates were left to Carlingford, 186-.

Martha Anne b. 1810, m. Rev. E. M. Hamilton (1802–61), of Brown Hall, Donegal.

Thomas (1815–1887; *o.s.p.*), cr. Lord Clermont (Irish peer 1852, U.K. 1866): m. 1840, Louisa Grace (1816–1896), 3rd d. of 1st Marquess of Ormonde.

Harriet (1824–89) a Catholic convert, 1877: m. 1854, David Urquhart (1805–77), M.P. Stafford 1847–52.

Chichester Fortescue, cr. Lord Carlingford (U.K.) 1874, succ. as 2nd Baron Clermont (Ireland) 1887, *o.s.p.* 1898: m. 1863 Frances, Lady Waldegrave (d. 1879).

Chichester Hamilton (1835–79.)

Martha Angelina, m. Revd. K. Stewart.

Several children.

INDEX

NOTES. Carlingford is referred to by the single letter C. throughout the index: since he appears so frequently a separate entry for him was impracticable. No references are given to the biographical notes on the individuals mentioned in the text of the journal which can normally be found appended to the first appearance of their names.

Hartington, Marquess of—(contd)
  on Egyptian finance, 56, 57; and reconquest of Khartoum, 61, 69, 89;
  on Suakin–Berber railway, 65 & n;
  in sharp exchange with Chamberlain, 69; and coalition, 72; speaks
  well in Sudan debate but votes for
  resignation in Cabinet, 73, 74;
  defends Wolseley's proposed proclamation, 79; snubs Harcourt, 92;
  and Anglo-Russian crisis, 92, 94;
  opposes 'Central Board' scheme, 98;
  attends meeting of Spencer's supporters, 102; on Radicals and Crimes
  Bill, 103; Queen on, 109; misses ministerial meetings, 116, 118, 119; on
  Gladstone, 123; speaks out against
  Parnell, 133, 140, 143 & n; also
  mentioned, 16, 29, 37, 58, 71, 76, 82,
  91, 97, 101, 122, 128, 139, 148, 156
Heneage, Edward, 111 & n, 128
Henniker, Miss Helen, 131
Herat, Afghan town, Russian advances
  on, 85, 92, 147
Heriot's Hospital, Edinburgh, 81,
  83 & n
Herschell, Sir F., 93, 118
Hibbert, J. T., 58
Hill, F. H., 78
Hohenlohe, Princess, 109
Holker Hall, Lancs., Gladstone at,
  80 & n
Home Rule, C.'s views on, 36–7
Huxley, T. H., 5, 121

Ignatiev, Count N. P., 86; British
  ambassador on, 148
Ipswich, Chamberlain's speech at, 51
Ireland, Cabinet delays discussion of,
  31–2; C. in, 83–4, 136–8
Irish Americans, 141
Irish Endowed Schools Bill (1885),
  137 & n, 138
Irish Land Act (1870), C.'s part in,
  11–12
Irish Land Purchase Bill (1885),
  Cabinet crisis over, 103, 105, 111;
  introduced by Tories, 127

Irish National League, see under
  National League below
Italy, C. in, 143

James, Henry, 63, 71, 72, 93, 120, 121,
  129, 132
Jedburgh, Roxburghshire, and Redistribution Bill, 113 & n
Jenkinson, E. G., on Home Rule,
  139
Joyce, Myles, 114

Keenan, Sir Patrick, 137–8
Kenmare, 4th Earl of, 71, 74
Kensington, 4th Baron, 67, 75, 128
Khartoum, fall of, 29, 33, 61, 80;
  Cabinet decide to recapture, 61–2,
  but leave its future government in
  doubt, 66, 69; Harcourt calls for
  abandonment of expedition to, 76;
  abandonment agreed to by Cabinet,
  89; extract from Wolseley's letter
  announcing fall, 148–9
Kimberley, Countess of, 75
Kimberley, 1st Earl of, as Wodehouse,
  10; sees Germany as unfriendly
  power, 47, 50; supports Gladstone's
  'unpatriotic' proposals on Egyptian
  finance, 53; on New Guinea, 56;
  gives strong support for reconquest
  of Khartoum, 62; predicts resignation on 28 Feb., 73, but votes to carry
  on, 74; criticized by wife, 75; and
  Anglo-Russian crisis, 76, 80, 92, 94,
  99–100; his journal cited, 89n, 112n;
  quarrels with Harcourt in Cabinet,
  92; reveals dislike of 'Central Board'
  scheme, 97, 100; attends meeting of
  Spencer's supporters, 102; acts as
  main Liberal spokesman for Redistribution Bill in Lords, 114, 116,
  118; extracts from letter received by,
  146–7; promoted Colonial Secretary
  1870 instead of C., 154, 157; also
  mentioned, 1, 2, 68, 72, 79, 105, 120,
  122, 125
Komaroff, Gen., victor of Penjdeh, 86,
  94